I0019215

Artificial Intelligence
in Journalism

Artificial Intelligence in Journalism

Changing the News

TONY SILVIA

McFarland & Company, Inc., Publishers
Jefferson, North Carolina

Library of Congress Cataloging-in-Publication Data

Names: Silvia, Tony, author.
Title: Artificial intelligence in journalism : changing the news / Tony Silvia.
Description: Jefferson, North Carolina : McFarland & Company, Inc., Publishers, 2025. | Includes bibliographical references and index.
Identifiers: LCCN 2024048626 | ISBN 9781476694085 (paperback : acid free paper) ∞
ISBN 9781476654829 (ebook)
Subjects: LCSH: Journalism—Technological innovations. | Artificial intelligence. | Journalism—Objectivity.
Classification: LCC PN4784.T34 S55 2025 | DDC 070.4/3—dc23/eng/20241023
LC record available at https://lccn.loc.gov/2024048626

British Library cataloguing data are available

ISBN (print) 978-1-4766-9408-5
ISBN (ebook) 978-1-4766-5482-9

Front cover image: © metamorworks/Shutterstock

Printed in the United States of America

*McFarland & Company, Inc., Publishers
Box 611, Jefferson, North Carolina 28640
www.mcfarlandpub.com*

TABLE OF CONTENTS

PREFACE

Close your eyes. Listen closely. What *don't* you hear as you enter that space once known as a newsroom? Maybe it's the *New York Times* or the *Washington Post*. Maybe it's CNN or NBC.

What's missing?

People. Reporters. Editors. Researchers. Storytellers.

Flash forward. It's now 2030. If the experts' predictions are correct, the silence is, to use a cliché that skilled writers try to avoid, deafening.

Where did all the voices go? Those magnificent purveyors of information that sometimes rose to the level of wisdom. The gaggle of, well, a "gaggle," that assembly of human beings bringing not only sound but also *voice* to an audience.

Maybe it wasn't one voice, but many voices, each unique, each bringing different perspectives to the same narrative. It is *narrated.*

Who does the narrating? The answer is a tale of then, now and next.

Each individual in that long-ago news space looked at what we once called facts through a unique lens, shaped by one's own experiences, skills, and talents. Yes, sometimes that lens would be discernibly blurred. Readers knew that. Viewers knew that. Or they used to think they did, because the trail that led to their consumption of information called "news" passed through human brains, hands, and hearts.

Accuracy, accountability, and trust—there's nothing artificial about any of those concepts. All, among others, are components of what we historically accept as major tenets of journalism.

Each depends upon the exercise of judgment. Traditionally,

that's where experienced editors and reporters come in. They provide not only knowledge but also context, connections that extend much farther than the distance between the finger and the keyboard—or at least when they do their job well.

It is not a mechanical process and, at its highest level, there is nothing artificial about it at all. It's born of time, experience, learning, adaptation and innovation. It encompasses information gleaned from the past but hopefully also adds to the repository of human knowledge.

But it's 2030 and the news space, what we once called a *newsroom*, is quiet, still, haunted, but for one brain stem, not really a brain, but a wholly different kind of space populated by the work of humans, but not, in and of itself, human at all.

We may call it artificial intelligence, but it is very much real, very much a part of the tapestry of art, science, medicine—and journalism. Its potential is enormous, its power seemingly infinite.

Journalists once *researched* the background to stories, first using previous stories written on a topic, maybe even books, often turning to a newspaper or broadcast station's archives (ironically referred to as the "morgue"). Artificial intelligence *scrapes* from information it's been given to formulate stories based upon a body of knowledge on any given topic, delivering, in some instances, a fully written, fully realized news story.

The term "scrape" itself suggests skimming the surface of a topic or story, but artificial intelligence proponents suggest otherwise. The argument goes that AI (the accepted abbreviation for artificial intelligence) can sift through millions, billions, potentially trillions of articles, reports, stories, records, an entire database of all the knowledge on any subject far faster and more efficiently than any human possibly can or could.

If it sounds like, to quote Huxley, a brave new world, it may well be—at least for AI's developers and the corporations that back them. But for journalists, what does AI mean? Does it increase accuracy, accountability, and trust in news media or dramatically reduce these things? Is it a useful tool, along with all the other, more traditional tools used by journalists in their quest for better storytelling, or can it add to the problem of mis- or disinformation already so prevalent in American society?

Beyond its potential and power, does AI have a downside? Does better or even somewhat improved journalism result from what is essentially a robotic process, or does an important part of developing and receiving information result from collaboration and the interaction of human neurons processing, judging, and balancing that information?

From the perspective of efficiency and economy of scale, AI and journalism would seem, from a corporate media standpoint, a perfect match: faster stories created at much less expense. But what might be lost in the process? Is that loss worth the gain?

As you read the pages ahead, keep in mind a central theme: these are not idle, academic questions, and the horizon on which they are posed is not distant. AI is now. It is and has been in our lives for much longer than any of us recognize: in our homes, in our cars, in nearly every aspect of what we say, see, and do. Why would or should journalism be any different?

Unbeknownst to you, it's highly possible, if not entirely probable, that you have already read, heard, or seen news stories that are completely created not by human brains and hands but by AI bots—a term that will be further defined shortly.

There is little wonder that some in the AI community refer to it as "the new internet," its rapid development outpacing the rise of the greatest, most powerful disruptive change in media and communication since Gutenberg invented the printing press.

Whether that claim is hyperbole or prophecy will be determined by how we use this technology and our vigilance as a society to ensure we don't abuse it. That process depends upon preparing the next generation of decision-makers, both journalists and their audiences, for a level of media literacy that's unprecedented.

In the upcoming chapters, many questions will be posed: important questions that might lead to some solutions surrounding AI's place in journalism and in democracy, with the underlying assumption that the two are critically connected at this point in America's history.

Preface

If artificial intelligence is the new internet, let's begin with the question of how we are wiring ourselves not only for the challenge that is here and now but also for the challenges that lie ahead.

INTRODUCTION

When I started in radio in the 1970s, the prevailing technology was something that recently has undergone a revival: vinyl records. Next were cartridges, plastic cases that housed the music, commercials, and jingles. We recorded our spots (advertisements) and our shows on tape, usually of the reel-to-reel variety. Today, all of the above are digitally produced, recorded, and distributed via computer.

When I started in television news, film had been the prevailing technology since the medium's inception in the 1940s. It evolved from its use in making motion pictures to this new medium of TV, not only in news but also in all forms of programming. Decades later, around the 1980s, videotape was introduced; there was a cry of protest from those whose skills were born and bred on film. Videotape evolved over the last few decades into digital storage of images, in everything from cameras to tablets to phones. Today, that's where news stories are recorded. Ultimately, they're delivered to the audience via a digital interface.

When I started in teaching in the late 1980s, videotape was still prevalent in teaching students how to shoot, write, and edit their news stories. Up until the early 2000s, I was still using video clips to illustrate some of my lessons. The classrooms were still equipped with combination VCR/DVD players, and the big technological leap was the addition of a projector that made it possible to put the image and sound on a big (formerly movie) screen in the front of the room (as opposed to rolling in a television set for playback). Today, videocassettes and DVDs, which in themselves were a big advancement from videotape, are gone, as is the hardware that accommodated them. Today, everything is housed on and disseminated through the hard drive of a classroom computer.

What's my point? *Change.* It's always the unknown. It's often scary. It's seldom easy.

In journalism, the "old guard" resists change, sometimes vehemently, often against its own best interests, and finds it hard to adapt. Radio did when television found its footing. Newspapers did when the internet gained prominence. Television is still trying to find its balance in regard to streaming.

And in the middle of all that change comes artificial intelligence. As the pages ahead will demonstrate, it's not new. It has been in our homes and cars and appliances long before we validated it with a "name." But that doesn't make it less the unknown, scary, hard tech pill to swallow.

In 2011, with my coauthor Terry Anzur, I published a book titled *Power Performance: Multimedia Storytelling for Journalism and Public Relations.* That seems eons ago in terms of advanced technology. It's hard to fathom now, but the term "multimedia" scared those in media, including journalism, because it threatened their jobs, their livelihoods, their entire careers. Today, it has become a benign term. Produce the same news story for more than one medium? Sure. It's expected. It's normal. It's accepted.

Will the same occur with artificial intelligence? That's the thrust of this book. In this moment, it's scary and unknown, and it makes at least some journalists feel temporarily incompetent. Like audiotape, videotape, digital cameras, the internet, and so many other technologies that have transformed our society and culture, AI is threatening precisely because it is "new." Journalism is not immune.

A friend and former colleague sent me a message as I was wrapping up this book, saying, "Seems like this one could be updated monthly with how quickly AI is evolving and journalism is (or is not!) adapting." That's the perfect way to introduce what you're about to read. In the case of AI, it's not only the seismic change but also the rapidity of that change that provokes both hope and fear among journalists and in society as a whole.

The hope is that the fear is unfounded. We begin with trying to understand what AI is (and isn't) and end with some commentary and predictions about its use in journalism from some of the most brilliant people I'm honored to know and whose insights on the future of AI in journalism are invaluable. In between, there are thoughts, conversations, research, and admonitions that may help drive the conversation of AI's proper place and usage in journalism and in the world.

One more thing: I wrote every word. None of it was written by an AI bot, except where, for illustrative purposes, it was. Because it is so difficult to distinguish between what is and isn't created by AI, transparency is at the center of all conversations involving artificial intelligence, now and in the future.

Chapter 1

A Brief History of Artificial Intelligence

Earliest Origins

What some now call the "new internet" actually dates back much further than the online world. Its earliest origins are traceable to England in 1951. Its earliest successful AI program was created at the University of Oxford—it was actually run on a system at the University of Manchester—by Christopher Strachey, who later became director of the university's Programming Research Group. It was so successful in simulating the processes of the human brain that a year later, Strachey's program was actually capable of playing a full game of checkers at what, for the time, was an amazing speed.

Even earlier, another British computer programmer, Alan Mathison Turing, had codified an abstract computing machine that not only had a limitless memory but was also capable of scanning throughout its own memory bank, reading what it found on a given subject, and creating new symbols. It was called the Turing "stored program concept," later referred to as the Turing Machine. Much later, it became the basis for our modern computers.[1]

While Strachey's later iteration of AI was demonstrated using the game of checkers, Turing's was even more sophisticated for its time. He used chess as the measure of how a computer could "learn" and solve complex problems. Turing created some primitive programs for playing chess using his "machine," but never one that was entirely successful. Still, the first "true" AI programs, those as we know them today, had to await the advent of "stored program electronic digital computers"[2]

In the United States, the first AI program also involved the game of checkers, perhaps because it involves a modicum of "thinking" as well as logic and predictability. Following up on Strachey's research, Arthur Samuel created a program in 1952 that was capable of playing checkers, but more importantly, his creation was expanded and refined a year later to add features enabling the computer to learn from its own experience in playing the game. That form of "learning" was a first step in what we now call "evolutionary computing." By 1962, Samuel's AI iteration was capable of winning a checkers game against a human opponent (and a recognized champion as well!).

These might have seemed amazing feats at the time, but they barely compare to the accomplishments yet to come. The early visionaries who saw its potential could never have envisioned both its progress and its acceptance and adoption, albeit sometimes cautiously, by the general public.

Here Come the Robots

While the 1950s and '60s were seminal in the development of the kinds of AI applications that have since come to fruition, the high cost of computers (estimated at the time in the vicinity of $200,000 per month), as well as the process of computing itself, stalled progress until the latter half of the twentieth century. Before 1949, computers were incapable of what Turing and others had yearned for in their research. They lacked a key component for "intelligence," that is, they couldn't store commands, only follow them.

However, progress on this front was steady, due in part to ongoing research by arms of the U.S. government specifically linked to intelligence, defense, and the military. As importantly, the whole idea of machines that could learn captured the imaginations of average everyday citizens, leading to the popularization, especially within the genre of science fiction, of robots that could think and act "like" humans.

As a Harvard study on AI states: "In the first half of the 20th century, science fiction familiarized the world with the concept of artificially intelligent robots. It began with the 'heartless' Tin Man from the *Wizard of Oz* and continued with the humanoid robot that impersonated Maria in *Metropolis*."³ This entry into popular culture solidified the idea—and to some extent the fear—that the day wasn't far off when robots would be able to do anything as well as a human, maybe even better in some instances. This form of humanoid, a thinking machine with vast and limitless possibilities, was both enticing and terrifying. While it might be amusing within the confines of entertainment, its logical extension into the realm of taking over society and the world in general was embedded in the public's earliest recognition of the promise and the peril of machines with infinite capacity to think, learn, and potentially "rule" the world.

As another observer put it: "When most people hear the term artificial intelligence, the first thing they usually think of is robots. That's because big-budget films and novels weave stories about human-like machines that wreak havoc on Earth. But nothing could be further from the truth."⁴ The truth is that since those earliest days, the development of AI has been so rapid that many experts, both inside and outside the field, suggest this "new" internet's pace of growth far exceeds and outpaces the advent of the internet itself. In an article titled "AI is the New Internet," Derick David posited: "Well, look at it this way. Internet at the moment is everywhere, right? In 10 years or less, AI will also be everywhere. From your iPhone, iPad, MacBook, SmartTV, public telescreens, and other devices. AI's effect on people will be of a much greater magnitude." The only flaw in this prophecy is that it didn't take ten years, but substantially less time; in fact, to date, the fastest time in the development of any medium.⁵

One reason for AI's rapid spread is its convenience. Another is commercialization. The two are linked to the extent that people will pay for convenience, and businesses, especially those in the tech industry, are willing to provide it—for a price.

So what does AI do for "us," the larger population? What do we need to know about how it works and how much do we *want* to know? Artificial intelligence has many meanings to many constituencies, but its basic functionality is most relatable in its application to our everyday lives, not only as journalists but also as citizens. For most

Americans and many around the globe, iterations of AI exist in our homes, in our cars and trucks, in our classrooms, our newsrooms, and even our hospitals. Beginning in 2023, much of our awareness of AI revolves around one program that has become the buzz word for AI: ChatGPT.

AI and ChatGPT: Algorithms and Anxiety

Before delving into what perhaps is the most recognizable (at least in terms of media reports) form of AI, it's useful to have a basic knowledge of AI and how it works. For our purposes, we'll focus less on the technical aspects and more on terms we all can recognize and, for the most part, use, beginning with the concept of algorithms, which drive so much of what we do online, on social media, and in doing business. In the simplest of terms, "AI refers to the simulation of human intelligence by software."[6]

More broadly,

- AI refers to the simulation or approximation of human intelligence in machines.
- The goals of artificial intelligence include computer-enhanced learning, reasoning, and perception.
- AI is being used today across different industries from finance to healthcare.

Among those industries is journalism specifically and media in general. The major components that drive AI are algorithms, computer code that searches for similarities between various concepts and draws comparisons between them, in order to create content. Whenever you search for a topic, product, or person, an algorithm compares your search with other "like" subjects or products, leading to suggestions for further exploration (or purchase). Search engines can already do exactly that, but the difference with AI is that its goal, as stressed above, is reasoning—learning and thinking like a human brain. AI can absorb and quickly analyze, compare, and collate infinite amounts of data, including text, images, and video.

Chapter 1. A Brief History of Artificial Intelligence

The major difference between what we've come to know as search engines like Google is that "artificial intelligence is based on the principle that human intelligence can be defined in a way that a machine can easily and mimic it, from the most simple to those that are even more complex. The goals of artificial intelligence include mimicking human cognitive activity." There are four types of AI:

- **Reactive AI** uses algorithms to optimize outputs based on a set of inputs. Chess-playing AIs, for example, are reactive systems that optimize the best strategy to win the game. Reactive AI tends to be fairly static, unable to learn or adapt to novel situations. Thus, it will produce the same output given identical inputs.
- **Limited-memory AI** can adapt to past experience or update itself based on new observations or data. Often, the amount of updating is limited (hence the name), and the length of memory is relatively short. Autonomous vehicles, for example, can "read the road" and adapt to novel situations, even "learning" from past experience.
- **Theory-of-mind AI** is fully adaptive and has an extensive ability to learn and retain past experiences. These types of AI include advanced chatbots that could pass the Turing Test, fooling a person into believing the AI was a human being. While advanced and impressive, these AI are not self-aware.
- **Self-aware AI**, as the name suggests, becomes sentient and aware of its own existence. Still in the realm of science fiction, some experts believe that an AI will never become conscious or "alive."[7]

As Frankenfield, who designated the above categories, states, "The applications for artificial intelligence are endless." He identifies the following:

AI is being tested and used in the healthcare industry for suggesting drug dosages, identifying treatments, and for aiding in surgical procedures in the operating room. Other examples of machines with artificial intelligence include computers that play chess and self-driving cars.

There are applications, as highlighted above, within the financial industry, where AI can be deployed to flag unusual banking activity, including a high level of debit card use or large deposits and withdrawals. That application can help identify instances of fraud. AI can also be used to make stock trading easier.

The application that has attracted the most attention (and debate) is a program named ChatGPT, which made its way into the mainstream in 2022. Most consumers identify artificial intelligence with ChatGPT. The two terms are nearly synonymous. However, ChatGPT makes up a very small percentage of the myriad ways AI is being used in our everyday lives.

So, what is ChatGPT and what are its implications for many fields, including journalism? The definition is easy, but the implications are far reaching and harder to predict. They include a strong potential impact not only on journalism but also on education, medicine, industry, and government.

AI's Major Player

Artificial intelligence came into the general public's consciousness in as recently as November 2022 through an AI program formally named Chat Generative Pre-trained Transformer, better known as ChatGPT. According to the website TechTarget, "ChatGPT is an AI chatbot that uses natural language processing to create humanlike conversational dialogue. The language model can respond to questions and compose various written content, including articles, social media posts, essays, code and emails."[8]

As such, it presents great promise, but also considerable concern in many of the fields mentioned. ChatGPT is a form of "generative AI," meaning it's a type of artificial intelligence technology that can produce various types of content, including text, imagery, audio and synthetic data. As Hetler, cited above, also observes, the recent buzz around generative AI has been driven by the simplicity of new user interfaces for creating high-quality text, graphics and videos.

This is where the nearly primal fear of AI begins, but it doesn't end here. In fact, at this writing AI is evolving so quickly that it's impossible to predict its next iteration. The maelstrom that

Chapter 1. A Brief History of Artificial Intelligence

ChatGPT has created by making its OpenAI program so widely and for the most part freely available to the public since its inception can be compared to the aforementioned fear of robots. In education, concerns over students turning in essays they didn't write, but instead generated through ChatGPT, has been rampant and vocal.

In industry, the fear of AI being capable of doing tasks better than humans, leading to job losses, is palpable and to some extent understandable. The ultimate fear mirrors the trepidation about robots that can think for themselves, creating a world in which humans are subservient to computers, with artificial intelligence becoming not only capable of creating text, audio, and video but also of correcting its own mistakes, teaching itself improvements, and becoming so perfect at any task that human intelligence can't begin to compete with its accuracy, efficiency, and efficacy.

But is AI capable of originality, of creativity? Should those of us who write books or articles, plays or poems be concerned that we can easily be replaced by an AI program that can write just as compelling screenplays, television scripts, novels, or any other form of imaginative, creative work? As of this writing in 2023, SAG (the Screen Actors Guild) and WGA (Writers Guild of America) jointly staged a strike because, among other concerns (such as residuals for streaming content), they want assurances that AI won't replace them in the future. It's a valid fear.

Think about it from an industry perspective. Computer programs like ChatGPT (the most dominant at this writing and the most recognizable, but only one of many) don't ask for royalties, vacations, workers' compensation, or health care. The biggest expense any employer faces is upgrades to the technology, but that's true of any technology, even at the consumer level with laptops, tablets, and cell phones. The savings to a corporation or organization, be it industry, education, healthcare, entertainment or, yes, journalism are potentially enormous. It's hard to argue against the economic benefits to cities, towns, states, nations, corporations and organizations, but what about the human side of the argument? Is there an upside to society as AI refines, expands, and proliferates? Should we collectively wring our hands in despair and stand strong against AI's progress, shivering at the thought of computers that can outpace and outthink us?

It's a human tendency to fear the new, but it is almost always the unknown that we truly fear. That fear is not unique to new technology, but a lot of it is centered on fear of the unknown. It's useful to recall that once did we not only fear robots, which now assemble, without eliminating human jobs, everything from cars to home appliances, radiation from cell phones and microwave ovens, to name just a few automated tasks. And recall that classroom teachers once feared (some still do) the potential for student cheating on essays linked to cut-and-paste technology made possible by programs like Microsoft Word. What about spell-check? It was going to lead to a society where no one could write or spell.

While that prophecy hasn't completely come true, the concerns were real. Is Alexa really listening to us every time we converse on a subject or discuss a product in the kitchen or living room? Is that how those same topics or products end up in our social media feeds? That has long been a debate. As for social media itself, is it a force for good or evil, connecting or dividing us? These are all questions and concerns that arise at the start of a new technology's advent and adoption. No doubt there were those (especially in the aristocracy of many nations) who feared Gutenberg's putting books in the hands of commoners via his invention of the printing press.

However, there may be specific reasons to beware of the burgeoning power of this new, powerful technology, if for no other reason than the rapid speed of its development. AI, if it *is* the new internet, has the potential, like its predecessor, to attract both good and bad players. In one of my favorite Shakespeare plays, Hamlet opines, "There is nothing good nor bad, but thinking makes it so." Applied to AI in its current form, it may be our own thoughts that frame the fear of a dystopian world where we cede control to a powerful, omniscient techno entity, removing our ability to choose or decide our own destinies.

The Good, the Bad, and the Ugly of AI

Many analyses of artificial intelligence's power focus not on the here and now, but on the future. There's a reason for that: the aforementioned rapidity of AI development is unprecedented—and daunting. No other technology, not the internet itself, neither the printing press nor electricity, has come so far, so fast. There are many who currently believe AI *must* be regulated, but some of the same prognosticators and pundits suggest it *can't* be regulated. Regulation of AI faces the same challenges as regulation of the internet, perhaps in some ways a well-intentioned task, but in the years since the internet's advent, how successful has that mission been? A similar question can be asked in regard to social media. The big questions persist: who does the regulating? Is it government? Is it the technology companies who invented AI?

Consider this. When was the last time you saw CEOs of major tech companies (or any mega corporations, for that matter) go to Capitol Hill and voluntarily ask Congress to regulate them and their business? That would be never. But it happened in 2023 when several of AI's biggest players, even some of its inventors, testified to a U.S. Senate committee studying artificial intelligence. Sam Altman, CEO of OpenAI, the company that makes ChatGPT, stated that government regulation "will be critical to mitigate the risks of increasingly powerful" AI systems. "As this technology advances, we understand that people are anxious about how it could change the way we live. We are too," Altman added.[9]

And he wasn't alone. As the *Washington Post* reported, "a trio of influential artificial intelligence leaders testified at a congressional hearing Tuesday, warning that the frantic pace of AI development could lead to serious harms within the next few years, such as rogue states or terrorists using the tech to create bioweapons." Lest this seem hyperbole, the same *Post* article goes on to report other concerns raised by mega-giants of the AI industry.

Yoshua Bengio, an AI professor at the University of Montreal, who is known as one of the fathers of modern AI science, said the United States should push for international cooperation to control the development of AI, outlining a regime similar to international rules on nuclear technology. Dario Amodei, the chief executive of AI start-up Anthropic, said he fears cutting-edge AI could be used to create dangerous virus and other bioweapons in as little as two years. And Stuart Russell, a computer science professor at the University of California, Berkeley, said the way AI works means it is harder to fully understand and control than other powerful technologies.

The timeline for AI's ability to not only replicate but to also improve upon human intelligence has these techno titans worried. The *Post* summarized the Senate hearing thusly: "The hearing demonstrated how concerns about AI surpassing human intelligence and getting out of control have quickly gone from the realm of science fiction to the mainstream. For years, futurists have theorized that one day AI could become smarter than humans and develop its own goals, potentially leading it to harm humanity."[10]

When asked, one of AI's earliest developers, Jim Goodnight, the man sometimes referred to as "the Godfather of AI," said even he was amazed at the pace of the technology's development. According to a 2019 report by CNBC, "He never imagined that the technology he created to improve crop yields would evolve into sophisticated data analytics software, a precursor to modern day AI. Back then computers could only compute 300 instructions a second and had 8K of memory. Today they can execute 3 billion instructions a second and contain multiple terabytes of memory."[11]

A more recent assessment in 2023 asked us to imagine the future, beginning now. It's a world where AI operates medical facilities, runs airlines, and even has the potential to mount legal prosecutions and defenses. Everything moves faster, costs less, but what about war? Can AI operate cyber weapons? It may seem unimaginable, but it's all too possible. AI is everywhere. With the promises come challenges that threaten to change everything from politics to global economies:

> The twenty-first century will throw up few challenges as daunting or opportunities as promising as those presented by AI. In the last century, policymakers began to build a global governance architecture that, they hoped, would be equal to the tasks of the age. Now, they must build a new

governance architecture to contain and harness the most formidable, and potentially defining, force of this era.[12]

AI regulation would appear to be at the center of the debate, but while U.S, regulators at least seem to have the will to listen, there doesn't appear to be a way to act, as the authors of the above study outlined in an MSNBC interview on that network's *Morning Joe* broadcast. Both the article and the interview point out that consortiums in other parts of the world have begun to address regulatory issues in a much more expansive and progressive manner. Perhaps because of regulatory agencies and Congress being reluctant to inhibit the development of what could, and probably will, become a major industry, the United States at this point lags behind Europe and other parts of the world in adopting rules and restrictions for AI. As with the internet, there are also here in the United States, much more so than in other nations, concerns over censorship issues. Still, when AI's progenitors ask for regulation to slow down their product, perhaps we should listen.

What's Journalism's Role?

Journalists are in a somewhat unique situation regarding the artificial intelligence revolution. While one major precept of the field is *objectivity,* one might ask how is that possible when reporting on AI. After all, many journalism organizations, as we shall see in the next chapter, already employ AI as a tool in researching and reporting news stories. Journalists also have a potential vested interest in how AI develops and what its capability ultimately becomes. As in other types of media, a highly sophisticated and developed AI program could spell the end to thousands of jobs in news media. Still, the debate over an ever-strengthening, increasingly powerful force like AI is a major news story.

The public, though they may not know much about the subject beyond the devices already equipped in their homes and cars, have a thirst for knowing more. Like science itself, however, information on AI is a moving target and even the most skilled specialists in any news organization, no matter the extent of their technological acumen, are hard pressed to keep up.

The dilemma is intensified by an age-old journalism question: How do you report on the story when, to some extent, you are part of the story? Journalists, like teachers, doctors, and workers in every other field, are compelled to develop expertise at lightning speed just to stay level with the power of AI in their own field, let alone report on the latest developments in other fields and the broader societal impact a tidal wave like AI will increasingly impose. Many, though not all, journalists embrace new technology and are often early adopters. How do you embrace technology that might one day lead to your own career demise?

It is not as if journalists and others in the media haven't faced this same situation before. Think about what's known as "voice-tracking" in the radio industry as a form of artificial intelligence. Of the over 15,000 radio stations in America, most use a computer program to generate what sounds like a live "voice." A radio station may not have a single employee present on-site. This is especially the case at night and during overnights when there are fewer listeners, but increasingly also at other times during the day.

It's essentially an everyday use of AI in media that saves station owners and media corporations large sums of money because the need is removed to hire a live host or newsperson. The public, for the most part, can't tell the difference because the process is so refined as to sound seamless to the human ear. The economic imperative is obvious, but what is lost, critics maintain, is a sense of localism or community. Could the same be done with news reports? It's already being done and has been for some time.

In some ways, these same challenges journalists face can foster unity with those in other fields whose concerns about AI in the workplace are similar. Many in the field of education fret over the possibility that AI will one day replace teachers in the classroom. As we discovered during the pandemic, having students learn online at home is an option across all grade levels, albeit with debatable results. But consider if AI could do the teaching, preparing the lessons, assignments, and tests. Think of the cost saving when school committees and boards realize that expensive school buildings are no longer necessary and teacher salaries are eliminated. The argument that human beings can teach better than AI becomes less compelling the more AI technology advances.

In medicine and health care, will doctors and nurses one day face elimination? Think about an AI program that can deliver a patient diagnosis in seconds by scanning and examining the entirety of knowledge related to that malady. If a doctor has never seen a certain kind of mole, for instance, or tumor, multiple rounds of testing can lead to months or years of patient discomfort and uncertainty. AI can potentially identify, diagnose, and recommend treatment in minutes. In other words, the job that it takes a human doctor or nurse weeks, months, or years to research, diagnose and treat could be accomplished by AI all in the same day.

Writing a book like this one takes months, if not years, when a human author is involved. AI can potentially produce the same book in a matter of hours or, at most, days. Should those of us who write books feel threatened? The argument is that in all forms of art, whether books, paintings, or music, human experience and creativity results in a better outcome, but is that true? Even if it is now, will it still be five or even two years from now? Will an AI program one day write a symphonic work equal to or even greater than Beethoven's Ninth? And the symphony orchestra members who perform that work, are they really necessary, since AI can be taught and ultimately can teach itself to reproduce every instrument in the ensemble?

Paintings take a long time, sometimes the better part of a lifetime, to produce by human hands. Who is to say that the next Rembrandt won't be produced between sunrise and sunset in a single day using AI? In the other visual arts, the same might be true. And if AI can create art and music, why can't it also be used to write television shows and movies, perhaps making the current objections to AI by the Screen Actors Guild and Writers Guild of America all too real? Actors, too, may become obsolete when, on an even higher level than current computer-generated images, AI can create bots capable of delivering lines like humans, gesticulating like humans, moving like humans, and telling the same stories more efficiently without the high salaries and (sometimes) egos human actors possess.

This may all sound speculative, an excursion into science fiction along the lines of some of Hollywood's most unlikely scenarios, but if we are to believe the founders of AI technology, it is a scenario neither futuristic nor fanciful. AI, with its myriad applications, is either a useful tool or a threat to all forms of human endeavor. Which brings us back to our central topic: journalism and its essential role in unraveling the maze of information and misinformation surrounding this burgeoning and revolutionary technology.

Is the role of journalists to inform the public without fear or favor, a phrase about journalism coined by Adolph Ochs, founder of the modern *New York Times*?[13] If so, then how does that apply to AI? Here, we may be talking about a very different kind of fear that Ochs's meaning: the fear journalists themselves have of their own extinction. After decades of well-documented newsroom job erosion, reporters and editors understandably wait for the next round of layoffs, mergers, and buyouts. The threat of AI to journalists' jobs, leading to the longer-term threat to journalism itself, makes it difficult for newsroom personnel to view AI through a lens that is entirely devoid of fear.

In some ways, the dilemma that journalists face in reporting on AI is similar to the challenges of reporting the Covid pandemic, i.e., they are charged with giving the public facts while also recognizing that, as human beings, they were threatened by the same existential threat as the public they served. In addition, the "facts," such as they are (and are in terms of AI), are fleeting, changeable, disputable, and non-foreseeable. On the other hand, that's what journalists must do: report without fear or favor. Mega multinational corporations have a stake in the future of AI technology (and many of those corporations have holdings in news organizations), which makes the challenge especially acute. The fact that reporters, editors, and news managers could put their own fates aside during Covid to do their best at informing the public suggests that reporting on AI might or should be equally selfless.

In many ways, however, the front lines of journalism, those

reporters and editors—and even news managers—who report the stories may be limited in their ability to analyze, scrutinize, and report upon this newest technological revolution. Even as individual journalists are doing due diligence by reporting the facts about AI, their ownership, often distant and disconnected from the newsrooms where they work, are working against them by employing AI to write many of the stories—about AI, among other subjects.

Artificial intelligence isn't a novel occurrence in today's newsrooms. It has been used to research, write, and distribute stories that readers and viewers may be unaware were neither seen nor touched by human brains or hands. It has not been a secret, but it also has not been widely known nor disseminated. The earliest use of AI in writing and reporting news presages the current awareness and concern over the AI medium itself, as we will see in Chapter 2.

Chapter 2

ARTIFICIAL INTELLIGENCE
ENTERS THE NEWSROOM

While the use of AI in journalism may appear to be a new practice, the reality is that newsrooms have been using this technology for at least a decade, with greater or lesser success. The venerable Associated Press (AP) was among the first to substantially experiment with the new medium's potential to produce news stories. Their own description of how and why they began using AI:

> Our foray into artificial intelligence began in 2014, when our Business News desk began automating stories about corporate earnings. Prior to using AI, our editors and reporters spent countless resources on coverage that was important but repetitive and, more importantly, distracted from higher-impact journalism.[1]

Their rationale seemed to focus on saving time on routine tasks and that the time saved could better be allocated to researching, writing, and disseminating longer-form stories, what they refer to above as "higher-impact journalism." This makes sense, considering that so many tasks performed by reporters and editors are indeed rote, and a tool that could, in a sense, automate those tasks would indeed save time and valuable resources. Consider, for instance, a long-established daily practice of calling police and fire departments to gain information about crimes, blazes, explosions, and other hazards. Traditionally, this task has been performed by a reporter or, in some instances, a newsroom intern. Using AI to make those calls and curate the information from them could be a very valuable time saver.

The AP, in fact, seems to have advanced the use of AI in news-gathering and reporting to a greater extent than other news organizations, which are only now, as of this writing in 2023–24, beginning to recognize AI's power and prioritize that power over the threat that it could pose if left unharnessed. On their website, they present a very coherent and transparent overview of how they employ AI technology. The array of both functional tasks and longer-term goals, like designing an online course teaching other newsrooms how best to use AI, is impressive if only to demonstrate how far AI in the newsroom has come in so brief a period of time. As proof of its commitment to AI exploration and innovation, as of 2024, as part of an ongoing initiative, AP had worked with local newsrooms to help them use AI not only to report but also to predict events, based upon data, as well as automating tasks like doing sports previews and game summaries and monitoring social media posts much more efficiently and providing story transcripts for broadcast media.

According to its own statistics, AP reaches four billion people, who see its stories in some form or on some platform, every day, in 100 countries and all 50 U.S. states: a powerful force indeed. Hence, it's not surprising that as an organization it has led the charge toward integrating AI into our nation's newsrooms. The fact that it has been integrated into so many facets of its news operation's master plan, as well spreading its use to other news organizations, is evidence of AP's early adoption, together with rapid technological improvements, translating to much more than reliance on a fleeting technology. Rather, it suggests that AI, unlike other forms of promising storytelling tools (virtual reality), is here to stay when researching, reporting, writing, producing, and disseminating news stories across all media platforms.

For that reason, among others, this revolutionary technology has captured the attention of the academic community, who has begun to delve into the analysis of AI's uses in newsroom settings. Before it was more popularly referred to in the short form of artificial intelligence, "AI," in 2020 an academic article described the phenomenon as "robot journalism." In "Integration or Replacement: Journalism in the Era of Artificial Intelligence and Robot Journalism," Saad and Issa postulated:

Perhaps one of the most important pivotal stations in the development of journalism in the world after the invention of printing was the technical uses of computers, which paved the way for qualitative changes that revolutionized all aspects of media process. A new idiom "Robot Journalism" was created recently, meaning the use of robots in making journalistic content.[2]

Saad and Issa predict that nine out of ten news stories would be written by robots by 2030. That statistic harkens back to the fears hearkens back to the comparison of AI with robots and the fear that the robots are destined to prevail through not only equaling but also surpassing human intelligence. Academics were not the first to compare AI in journalism to "robot" reporting.

The *New York Times* published a piece in 2019 titled "The Rise of the Robot Reporter," in which it stated that "journalism generated by machine is one the rise," adding the example of Bloomberg News:

Roughly a third of the content published by *Bloomberg News* uses some form of automated technology. The system ... is able to assist reporters in churning out thousands of articles on company earnings reports each quarter. The program can dissect a financial report the moment it appears and spit out an immediate news story that includes the most pertinent facts and figures.

In addition, the *Times* lists AI-generated stories on minor league baseball for the Associated Press, earthquake stories for the *Los Angeles Times*, and political contribution stories involving incumbent office holders. Moreover, the *Times* story pointed out that "in addition to covering company earnings for Bloomberg, robot reporters have been prolific producers of articles on minor league baseball for the Associated Press, high school football for the *Guardian*."[3]

Stages of AI Development in Newsrooms

Francesco Marconi, quoted in an article titled "Are We Entering the Age of Artificial Intelligence Journalism?," identified three stages in AI's emergence into journalism: automation, augmentation, and generation. Stage one involves freeing journalists from routine, repetitive tasks, allowing time for more quality investigative reporting; stage two emphasizes AI's use in analyzing massive amounts of data, video, and text to zone in on trends and patterns in stories over long periods of time.

The third and current phase, where we are as of this writing, "is driven by the AI generative movement, powered by large language models, which are capable of generating narrative text at scale." That means training programs like ChatGPT, discussed in Chapter 1, "to learn the patterns and structures of language to make educated guesses based on the words you've typed previously." AI is good at repetitive tasks, and, as such, ChatGPT can "be used to assist journalists to write short news stories or compile coverage of local weather and traffic."[4]

The increased computational power of today's AI programs, some of them cited above, is both fascinating and terrifying. In the generative phase, AI is projected to write, as in "generate," news stories on its own, devoid of human involvement. This is the phase of AI that scares today's journalists the most, from a loss of jobs perspective, as well as ethical concerns about accuracy and the spread of misinformation, a topic that will be discussed in detail in Chapter 8. For now, let it suffice to say that it is a valid concern, from both perspectives. Apart from journalists, the dimensions of this conversation have critical and far-reaching consequences for the public, most of whom have no idea that many of the news stories they now read or view on a daily basis are generated by AI, with little or sometimes no intervention from humans. Here are a couple from the Associated Press:

> TYSONS CORNER, Va. (AP)—MicroStrategy Inc. (MSTR) on Tuesday reported fourth-quarter net income of $3.3 million, after reporting a loss in the same period a year earlier.
>
> MANCHESTER, N.H. (AP)—Jonathan Davis hit for the cycle, as the New Hampshire Fisher Cats topped the Portland Sea Dogs 10–3 on Tuesday.

Granted, neither the above are potential Pulitzer Prize–winning stories. They more commonly represent the category of news pieces that are routine, showing that AI in the newsroom can be more an ally than an enemy, relieving human journalists of the burden often placed upon them to do rote stories that consume time, energy, and resources that might be better allocated.

Trial and Error in AI

The entry of AI technology into newsrooms has been a process of trial and error, fits and starts, as with most new technologies. Some innovations have brought cautious praise from various sectors, including from within the field of journalism itself. Some, like the Associated Press, have taken a slow but steady deliberate and thoughtful approach to implementing AI into its daily operations. Others have brought not praise but criticism from newsroom colleagues, including one in particular. In 2022, CNET, a website that publishes reviews, news, blogs, and podcasts, plus videos on technology and consumer electronics, dabbled in using AI to write news stories, beginning with those centered on business and financial stories. By all accounts, it was an unqualified disaster, causing CNET to backpedal amid a storm of backlash. Mainstream news outlets like the *Washington Post* emblazoned a headline in 2023, calling CNET's low-key entry into AI a "journalistic disaster."

The *Post*, among other news outlets, identified the essential problem: the 70 or so stories written completely using AI contained numerous errors, instances of plagiarism, and some mistakes that can only be labeled as dumb. The rival tech site Futurism cited a series of articles "filled with bonehead errors that drag the concept of replacing human writers with AI down to earth." One specific example given is a story about how compound interest is accrued.

To calculate compound interest, use the following formula:

Initial balance (1+ interest rate / number of compounding periods) ^ number of compoundings per period × number of periods

For example, if you deposit $10,000 into a savings account that earns 3% interest compounding annually, you'll earn $10,300 at the end of the first year.

According to Futurism's analysis, "It sounds authoritative, but it's wrong. In reality, of course, the person the AI is describing would earn only $300 over the first year. It's true that the total value of their principal *plus* their interest would total $10,300, but that's very different from earnings—the principal is money that the investor had already accumulated prior to putting it in an interest-bearing account." They go on to quote another expert on the cause of the error: "It is simply not correct, or common practice, to say that you have 'earned' both the principal sum and the interest," said Michael Dowling, an associate dean and professor of finance at Dublin College University Business School.[5]

The *Washington Post* agreed on AI's value and on the threat to human journalists. When entire stories are AI generated, it creates the impression that "the bots have betrayed the humans. Specifically, it turns out the bots are no better at journalism—and perhaps a bit worse—than their would-be human masters."[6] Again, we see the prevalence of traditional news media's initial trepidation that bots might be better at their jobs, but the mistakes AI made in about 1 percent of CNET's stories suggested that human intervention was essential in storytelling—as was full disclosure of the methodology used to generate those stories. As with any new technology, the mistakes made, once discovered and analyzed, led to an internal need to improve, not remove, the technology itself.

CNET pledged to do better. In January 2023, the site told readers not only how the AI mistakes occurred but also what they planned to do to prevent their recurrence. That included having human editors carefully expand their scrutiny of story drafts before they were published. Rather than restricting the time writers and editors have to review stories, CNET promised to give them more time to scan for factual errors.

Finally, in terms of moving forward, CNET stated its intention to continue using AI with certain caveats aimed at operational and editorial improvement:

> We're committed to improving the AI engine with feedback and input from our editorial teams so that we—and our readers—can trust the work it contributes to... In the meantime, expect CNET to continue exploring and testing how AI can be used to help our teams as they go about their work testing, researching and crafting the unbiased advice and fact-based reporting unbiased and factual reporting we're known for.[7]

Whether this journalistic mea culpa will satisfy all of CNET's critics is yet to be seen. Much will depend upon delivery of the promises made, but their initial endeavor into AI, while not without many discernible errors, may be ultimately viewed as no more nor less than the public and private price paid by those who are among the first to use new technologies.

Other Potholes on the Road to AI in the Newsroom

Errors of fact accruing from the earliest use of AI in newsrooms is not, and has not, been limited to American news organizations. As *Columbia Journalism Review* pointed out, *"La Libre,* a Belgian newspaper, reported that a man died by suicide after talking with a chat program called Chai; based on statements from the man's widow and chat logs, the software appears to have encouraged the user to kill himself." It appears that one of the paper's reporters tried the app, which is powered by an AI engine that uses an open-source version of ChatGPT, and it offered "different methods of suicide with very little prompting."[8]

A BuzzFeed reporter also captured attention when one of its reporters used a version of ChatGPT to create an opinion story that inadvertently praised Hitler, proposed solving San Francisco's homeless problem by shooting homeless people, and also, perhaps most incendiary, used the n-word. There were no human guardrails in place to catch the errors of both fact and judgment, leading to ethical as well as editorial decisions, the subject of Chapter 8, where we discuss a series of AI errors, misinformation and intentional hoaxes.

Consider the following errors found by the *Washington Post* and disseminated broadly by the *Columbia Journalism Review*'s Matthew Ingram:

> The original ChatGPT invented a sexual harassment scandal involving Jonathan Turley, a law professor at George Washington University, after a lawyer in California asked the program to generate a list of academics with outstanding sexual harassment allegations against them. The software cited a *Post* article from 2018, but no such article exists, and Turley said that he's never been accused of harassing a student.
>
> When the *Post* tried asking the same question of Microsoft's Bing, which is powered by GPT-4 (the engine behind ChatGPT), it repeated the false claim about Turley, and cited an op-ed piece that Turley published in *USA*

Today, in which he wrote about the false accusation by ChatGPT. In a similar vein, ChatGPT recently claimed that a politician in Australia had served prison time for bribery, which was also untrue. The mayor has threatened to sue OpenAI for defamation, in what would reportedly be the first such case against an AI bot anywhere.

Ingram also adds this to the roster of AI mistakes and transgressions:

> According to a report in *Motherboard*, a different AI chat program ... recently came under fire for sending sexual messages to its users, even after they said they weren't interested.... ChatGPT, for its part, has invented books that don't exist, academic papers that professors didn't write, false legal citations, and a host of other fictitious content.[9]

The *Arizona Republic*, a legacy newspaper, was not immune to inaccuracy in AI-generated stories. Like the Associated Press and other news outlets, the *Republic* used AI programs to do relatively simple, rote tasks like updating high school sports scores and reporting the final outcomes. Unfortunately, while not as potentially damaging as the examples cited above, nevertheless the process led to embarrassing results. Even when things went right, the writing fell short. When things went wrong, social media users noticed that odd phrases like "close encounters of the athletic kind" cropped up in story after story—a phrase that doesn't make sense to begin with but is even worse when repeated.

While the ethical standards of papers like the *Columbus Dispatch* say that "AI-generated content must be verified for accuracy and factuality before use in reporting," Axios reported that in at least one case, a story was published that had clear placeholders for "[[WINNING_TEAM_MASCOT]]." *PR Daily* concluded that, at the very least, this was a public relations failure, in addition to a journalistic one, suggesting that "like most industries, journalism is trying to figure out how to fit AI into its workflow. Unlike some other industries, they're often doing it in a very public way where failure is immediately evident."[10]

These very public errors, once pointed out by others within and outside the field, are reminiscent of a long-standing trope in journalism surrounding knowledge of how sausage is made: pulling back the curtain and showing the unpleasant and sometimes even nasty way that what we consume, in this case news and information, is made. There is little that most of us in any profession fear more than having our competence, credibility, or credulity exposed in public, but the irony in this instance is that so much of the controversy and fear surrounding AI and its applications in journalism have thus far been traceable not to the human imperfections of those who employ AI technology, but to shortcomings in AI itself. How long will these blips on the way to AI's refinement last? If, as outlined in Chapter 1, AI is developing at the rapid pace all of its developers predict—and fear—it won't be very long.

"The terror is right here in this [news]sroom"

No less a luminary than the man credited as "the father of broadcast journalism," Edward R. Murrow, knew the fear associated with new technology. At every stage of media evolution, changes in technology brought fear, some might even suggest terror, to those habituated to a previous, older form of technology. Newspapers feared radio. Radio feared television. Television feared cable. Cable feared the internet. Today, every medium that doesn't stream fears streaming. Have those fears proven to be valid? Perhaps, but all the forms of technology mentioned, each once-new technology, is still with us—albeit looking and functioning very differently today than at their inceptions.

Murrow had some very real fears surrounding the advent of this new technology called television and expressed those misgivings at a speech to the Radio-Television News Directors Association in 1958. In that speech, he referred to an "abiding fear" over not the use, but the potential misuse of the new television technology. "This instrument can teach, it can illuminate; yes, and even it can inspire. But it can do so only to the extent that humans are determined to use it to those ends. Otherwise, it's nothing but wires and lights in a box. There is a great and perhaps decisive battle to be fought against ignorance, intolerance and indifference. This weapon of television could be useful," he told his assembled audience of news managers and corporate executives.[11]

Chapter 2. Artificial Intelligence Enters the Newsroom

As a journalist, Murrow was never known to be recalcitrant when approaching a new technology—or a news story. The only other time he alluded to "fear" was when threatened not by the medium, but the message: in this instance Senator Joseph McCarthy's chilling effect on a program in which Murrow criticized the junior senator's Communist witch hunt. Sponsors boycotted the program, but Murrow forged ahead, even paying for ads in the *New York Times* out of his own pocket. When the final moment of broadcast came, he looked around the room at the other journalists assembled and famously said, "The terror is right here in this room."

It was an extraordinary statement from such an exalted journalist, but when combined with the RTNDA speech, it may reveal something about the nature of fear that accompanies any new intrusion—human or technological—into the newsroom culture, a culture that has its own rituals, codes, and fears—especially in the current media age of job losses linked to the pandemic and its aftermath, as well as the profit-driven motives of corporate media ownership that salivates at the thought of lower costs and higher profits. Contrary to some of the public's cynical view of journalists, they are *people*, needing to pay the rent and put food on the table like anyone else. Anything that threatens those human needs, be it the threat of advertiser withdrawal or an upstart technology that, if misused, could take over not only individual jobs but also the whole profession of journalism, becomes a major concern. That was as true in Murrow's day as it is today.

Could this be one reason why, in some of today's newsrooms, the real terror is less about how AI is used and more related to the fact that it is used at all? The major fear in news organizations may very well equate to what journalists see as the potential dehumanization of the craft of journalism itself, or, as the *Columbia Political Review* suggests, "It isn't the fear of technological assistance and its rapid advancements that haunt journalists. Rather, what is most concerning for journalists is the concept of 'artificial general intelligence,' which essentially is shorthand for a machine 'that can do anything the human brain can do.' Can creativity and empathy, two essential traits necessary for becoming a journalist, truly be automated by AI?"[12]

The Creativity Argument

In many ways journalists' argument surrounding the loss of creativity and empathy mirrors that of the Writers' Guild of America members who went on strike in 2023.

The essence of the argument remains that no matter how fast, efficient, or even accurate AI might be in creating narratives, even artificial generalized intelligence, AI's highest level, can never approximate, duplicate, or replace how humans feel, create, and inspire. The discussion of creativity, what it is, the role it plays in imaginative and artistic works, and whether it can be taught, instilled, or otherwise promulgated is an age-old debate, modernized by the entry of AI.

Writing in *Forbes* in 2023, Bernard Marr studied "the intersection of AI and human creativity" and posed the question: "Can machines really be creative?" While looking at creativity through a traditional lens, Marr suggests, "The ability to be creative has always been a big part of what separates human beings from machines. But today, a new generation of 'generative' artificial intelligence (AI) applications is casting doubt on how wide that divide really is!" The newest AI programs, he posits, can create a painting or write a song, a play, a novel, any form of creative human endeavor faster and more efficiently than a human writer, artist, author, or musician can. Is the work as good? That's the essential question: whether what computers can do with what humans give them in fact constitutes creativity. And what role does originality play in creativity?

In an argument that most closely parallels that of journalists, relative to their fear of marginalizing the humanity inherent in the best journalism, Marr outlines what might be absent in even the best AI-generated stories: "Human ideas and imagination often come from making connections—we see, hear, feel, or learn something, and this causes us to form an idea or opinion. When we express this by creating something that represents that connection—such as writing a poem about something sad in order to communicate the sadness of an event or situation to others—we are being creative in a very human way."[13]

Chapter 2. Artificial Intelligence Enters the Newsroom

A 2023 *Harvard Business Review* article took the approach that AI isn't best used as a replacement for human creativity, but as a way to augment it: "There is tremendous apprehension about the potential of generative AI—technologies that can create new content such as text, images, and video—to replace people in many jobs. But one of the biggest opportunities generative AI offers is to augment human creativity and overcome the challenges of democratizing innovation." This latter term, "democratizing innovation," suggests that AI could actually help everyday citizens explore their own potential and actualization of creativity by empowering them to be part of the process of making and innovating new creative endeavors. According to the *Review*'s author:

> MIT's Eric von Hippel ... since the mid–1970s, has been researching and writing about the potential for users of products and services to develop what they need themselves rather than simply relying on companies to do so. In the past two decades or so, the notion of deeply involving users in the innovation process has taken off, and today companies use crowd sourcing and innovation contests to generate a multitude of new ideas.[14]

In other words, the potential for more people to have direct input into the creative process may lead to innovation in many fields. According to this argument, creativity is enhanced, not stunted, by AI. It's interesting to note that journalists' reactions to AI runs the gamut from fear to fascination. One article discussing the AI creativity debate strongly argues that preconceptions about AI squelching creativity are rooted in a fallacy. Some philosophers believe that ChatGPT and programs like it will diminish our abilities to do better, higher-level work.

Instead, Columbia Business School professor Sheena Iyengar cites the example of how, in 1997, a computer program beat the seemingly invincible grandmaster Gary Kasparov in chess. That led to the fear that humans would never again master the game of chess, but the opposite happened. By studying the computer's moves, human chess players actually improved at playing the game. In addition, one study, quoted by Iyengar, concluded that "the presence of the non-human made the human a better, more creative player."[15]

The debate surrounding machine intelligence vs. human

creativity will not be one that's easily settled, since, like many issues, there are passionate and committed believers on both sides of the question. On the other hand, progress toward the increased use of artificial intelligence in our newsrooms, both general AI and generative AI, will only accelerate. In fact, there is some reason to believe that while AI may initially disrupt society and its norms, in the long term it could prompt a return to more human connectivity and creativity, not less.

The hope is that as AI develops, its presence in our newsrooms will be seen more as an ally, rather than an enemy. In some ways that may mean newsrooms that look less like anything at any time since the pandemic, integrating automated AI processes with human creativity. The question may very well become one of balance. Does AI augment human creativity or does human creativity directly influence AI's capacity to do more than it already does? In the next chapter, we will attempt to visualize what a "new" news organization might look like once the AI revolution hits full stride.

Chapter 3

Visualizing the AI Newsroom of the Future

In and of itself, the term "newsroom" is quickly becoming an anachronism. With the pandemic causing so many journalists to work remotely, the concept of a newsroom, a designated physical space where reporters, editors, photographers, and news managers gather to make decisions about what stories to cover, how to cover them, and deliberate over key editorial and ethical choices, is nearly absent in many news organizations. There are those who suggest that's not entirely a bad thing, citing the "old boys" culture that permeated so many newsrooms for decades. There are others who suggest that the traditional newsroom has to die in order for journalism to survive. The *New York Times*'s Maureen Dowd, quoted in an article about how much newsrooms need to change, recalls "the magic of the newsroom—the collaboration, the mentorship, the camaraderie [I] enjoyed—is inseparable from the culture of late nights, obsessive overwork, heavy drinking, and volatile personalities. But those factors have also made newsrooms hostile places for many journalists and editors—spaces that tolerate the brashest personalities and blatant favoritism."[1]

The Poynter Institute, a journalism think tank, began to track the demise of the traditional newsroom during the pandemic, documenting layoffs, furloughs, buyouts, mergers, advertising shortfalls, and total shuttering of news organizations numbering in the thousands across every U.S. state. Many of those job losses were permanent. Thus, the seeds of the traditional newsroom's slow march toward death may have been sown during the pandemic, but they grew rapidly in its aftermath. Older journalists' nostalgia for the legacy newsroom is understandable, but borders on misguided. As Bruce Springsteen famously wrote in "My Hometown" about steel mill jobs, "These jobs are going, boys, and they ain't coming back."

Increasingly, there are calls for change in the very fabric of our newsrooms, only hastened by the nearly three years of changes in journalism itself, necessitated by the pandemic. On the one hand, British journalist and tech writer John Crowley acknowledges how "newsrooms are an essential but romanticized part of our industry fabric." On the other hand, he is among many who suggest it may be time for "a once-in-a-generation transformation of the way journalists work."[2]

What would that transformation look like? What impact does the entry of artificial intelligence have on those spaces we once (and still colloquially) refer to as "newsrooms?" Does AI present an opportunity to reconfigure not only the physical space but also the process of news gathering, reporting, editing, and, most importantly, disseminating information to audiences? Is it just another tool in the journalist's toolkit, or can it play a transformative role as news organizations scramble to survive in a media landscape saturated with other choices?

The Functional and Cultural Value of AI to Today's Newsroom

AI in its current form is a bit like what was once called "computer-assisted reporting." Far from being integrated into the workflow of journalists in newsrooms (and even often physically far from the newsroom itself), the first generation of CAR was viewed with suspicion by traditionalists. One interesting irony is that journalists constantly report on change of one kind or another, but sometimes resist change in their own workplaces. It's easy to forget that when computers first entered the newsroom, many reporters and editors clung to their typewriters and copy paper. They were so divorced from the main workflow of the newsroom that computers were often situated in a computer "lab," near the frenzy of reporter and editor activity, but not a part of the overall operation. There were some in yesterday's newsrooms who bemoaned their arrival so vehemently that they refused to go near the great technological unknown across the room or down the hall, leaving their operation to the tech people who seemed a world apart from journalism.

Slowly, though, computers traversed the newsroom to reside prominently within the reach and view of news managers, reporters, editors, and photographers. The culture changed, but slowly. Why? Because it became necessary. Workplace efficiency and economic efficacy meant that the first iteration of newsroom computerization was not a choice, but a mandate. Together with the internet, the value of computers became both functional and cultural, making them what they are today: an indispensable part of the newsgathering process. There's reason to believe that in the 2020s, the same could become true for AI.

Rather than a traditional pod-like approach common to so many physical newsroom spaces, the goal would be to integrate AI into the functionality of all editorial tasks. Rather than have an AI "department," which would create silos among news workers, AI should be part of every newsroom function as we go forward toward visualizing and, eventually, actualizing a new kind of newsroom, one we might rename a "news space."

In the previous chapter, the fears of AI were made apparent, but what of the very real, very significant advantages AI can bring to the process of journalism? They are many potential ways AI could improve our news "spaces," as identified in a 2023 Harvard study cited in Chapter 2. They include the capacity to:

- promote divergent thinking
- challenge expertise bias
- assist in idea evaluation
- support idea refinement
- facilitate collaboration with and among users

In many ways, each of the above are the building blocks of a new AI-integrated news space. Considered first individually, and then collectively, the functional tasks above may represent AI's highest and best use.

Divergent Thinking

Traditional newsrooms can and often have fallen into the trap of consensus thinking. If you have ten journalists in a room, the ideas generated surrounding stories, photographs, or ideas in general may conform to what has been the norm, what has been successful in the past. Those on a lower level of the newsroom flowchart may be reluctant to come up with new ideas for fear that senior people would either be threatened by those ideas or shoot them down entirely. The potential for AI to remove this barrier to new and innovative ideas surrounding everyday journalism discussions is significant. It is also somewhat quantifiable. For one, the authors of the aforementioned Harvard study suggest that "generative AI can support divergent thinking by making associations among remote concepts and producing ideas drawn from them." They cite as an example "a text-to-image algorithm that can detect analogical resemblances between images, to generate novel product designs based on textual prompts from a human ... ultimately to create an image that combined an elephant and a butterfly, and it produced the chimera we dubbed 'phantafly' (sic)."

While this visual rendition more resembles a marketing tool than a journalistic one, it does illustrate the ability of AI programs to detect, recognize, and simplify similarities between seemingly disparate ideas and concepts that might escape the human brain. This capability, if ethically employed, could create a way for journalists to quickly and efficiently search for trends in all kinds of areas: at the macro levels of government, politics, crime, law, medicine, and science, and at the micro level similar trends across a range of local communities. Because algorithms lack ego, the hesitancy to bring up new ideas or spotlight certain trends is potentially minimized in a journalism setting. To the same degree, so might bias.

Expertise Bias

Today's journalists, perhaps more than at any other time in our collective history, are aware of the need to fight the public's perception that stories are constructed to feed and maintain the bias present not only in the individual journalist but also in journalism itself. Expertise bias might be defined as the tendency of journalists to rely entirely on their own areas of expertise and experience, as well as that of a few others—a narrowly defined and codified group of "experts"—to interview for their stories. The ability to think beyond one's own preconceived areas of expertise is a challenge for many journalists. Not so for AI. Preconceptions are not indigenous to algorithms; therefore, AI programs may help identify new avenues for exploration between one's own preconceptions and biases of what a story is and whose perspectives within that story are essential. As the Harvard study's authors put it: "This approach can lead to solutions that humans might never have imagined using a traditional approach, where the functions are determined first and the form is then designed to accommodate them."

Idea Evaluation

Journalists often inform their audiences about everyday consumer issues that directly affect their lives and lifestyles. AI may also be a valuable assistant in producing stories of this type. A story on food consumption might use AI to pinpoint ways to reduce, if not minimize, food waste. That leads to consumer awareness, but also to potential changes in the food industry itself. ChatGPT was able to examine how expiration dates affect the actual shelf life of food products, which led to manufacturers changing their approach to production, making smaller batches of food and replenishing their products more often on grocery store shelves—a plus for shoppers, but also for the industry itself.[3]

That's the kind of demonstrable change that journalists seek, but the research alone could consume months, if not years, while AI can assimilate, access, aggregate, and analyze the data needed to tell the story in a fraction of the time. When done properly, these kinds of stories create *impact*, one of the major tenets of good journalism.

Idea Refinement

In staying with the food waste analysis, ChatGPT was used to refine the idea to include other components that are equally valuable to the public, including the idea that creating dynamic expiration dates help reduce food waste, an app that helps consumers donate food that's nearing its expiration date, and educating users on how to make better and more informed decisions about when to buy and consume food. While not a solution to every story about a pressing societal problem, just this one program, ChatGPT, the most recognized and utilized AI program among many currently in use or in development, can be a major boost for journalists searching for a way to synthesize many elements of a story into a coherent and useful whole.

By assimilating seemingly disparate approaches to the same problem, AI helped create a solution to the problem of food waste. That's the kind of story that the public desires to read and that, with the help of AI, journalists can more easily provide. It also is a harbinger of how AI, properly understood and sensibly deployed, can be a collaborative partner in the process of many fields, journalism included.

Facilitate Collaboration

Not only does the journalist–AI collaboration hold great promise, but the collaboration with users outside the news space—audiences of every platform—also exists. News organizations are always searching for ways to engage users in stories. AI could be a solution. By giving readers/viewers/users the AI tools needed to collaborate not only with journalists but also with each other, the process of storytelling can only benefit. Crowdsourcing of stories has been an underutilized resource in journalism for years, but AI could bring a new level of collaboration. As the Harvard study authors put it, "the technology makes co-creation of new offerings much easier and less expensive. For example, a business can give users access to tools to generate designs and then create a personalized version of the product based on the customer's preferences." While some journalists still resist seeing journalism as a business, the fact remains that it *is* a business, and one that increasingly depends on technology for its survival.

With that in mind, it may be useful to look not at the naysayers of AI in journalism, but at those news organizations that are embracing this technology and using it to good advantage. They exist not only here in the United States but also around the globe, and, collectively, they help demonstrate early success in AI integration with the process of reporting and editing. They also demonstrate that the fear of losing journalism jobs to AI, while very real, may also be very exaggerated. In some instances, AI and those journalists who learn how best to use it may find a path to job preservation, not elimination.

Fighting the Fear

It may not be surprising that during the Covid pandemic, news organizations' use of AI experienced an uptick. In 2021, the *Columbia Journalism Review* launched a study to determine how news organizations were using AI specifically to report on the pandemic.[4] Their findings were interesting and may point toward the way toward AI's highest and best use in journalism. "More and more outlets experimented with the technology to help with things like reporting on COVID-19 case numbers, getting text messages out to readers, and more," the study concluded. Specifically, CJR's Samuel Danzon-Chambaud explained that "this type of structured data that can fit into predictable story frames lays the groundwork for automated journalism, a computational process that creates automated pieces of news without any human intervention, except for the initial programming." The news organizations in the study used automated journalism to quickly create texts, message boards, newsletters, photos, and videos at a time when information was changing rapidly. AI helped journalists "keep up: with a situation that required updating almost by the minute."

An organization named RADAR (Reporters and Data and Robots) partnered with Google even before the pandemic, in 2018, and its early embrace of AI allowed the tech company to provide data-driven, AI-generated articles to news outlets throughout England and Ireland at a critical time. RADAR "blends human editorial skills with the automation tech to create quality content quickly and on a massive scale." In the first 18 months of its operation, RADAR filed a quarter of a million AI-generated stories.[5]

Another news organization, KPCC-LAist, used AI to great advantage to increase community engagement during the pandemic and in other breaking news stories, including the California wildfires. They worked with an organization named Quartz, using AI to sift through an incredible number of readers' questions, organizing them by topic, theme, and even identifying trends in what the community most wanted to know.

In one example, Caitlin Hernandez, a KPCC-LAist assistant producer, explained how the service helped a reader:

> One question asker recently shared that she'd never heard of LAist until she was googling how to find answers to her COVID-19 questions. When we not only provided a space to ask but also a quick response, she found herself coming back to the site over and over—now saying she won't go anywhere else for essential news. Far from creating skepticism or distrust in readers, the site might actually experience the opposite: a stronger relationship leading to both loyalty and confidence in the news source itself.[6]

The Reynolds Journalism Institute experimented with using AI to edit the draft of a story. Journalist Maggie Doheny utilized the AI program Hemingway for the AI edit and then compared that version to one edited by a human in the newsroom. While the AI program helped spot some errors, like passive voice and hard-to-understand sentences, she also asserted that "an AI editor can't determine newsworthiness and doesn't provide any restructuring ideas or see where you need more context or sources. Not only that, it won't delete repetitive parts that may be unnecessary—a major role of an editor is to help your copy become more clear and concise." Her overall conclusion: "Tools like this could be useful for reviewing the first draft to catch the basics. Once writers have made those adjustments, it could then be passed on to the real-life editor for the final pass."

Examples abound of AI's positive use by news organizations. The news service Reuters, for one, has invested heavily in the technology, with great results. Data journalism is a growing field and it often mines important stories, but the downside is that analyzing large sets of data, identifying trends, and so on is both time consuming and costly. Reuters uses an AI system named News Tracer to beat the competition on major stories around the globe. According to its executive editor for editorial operations and data innovation, "since we started keeping analytical records about a year ago, Reuters News Tracer has beaten global news outlets in breaking over 50 major news stories.... This has given our journalists anywhere from an 8- to 60-minute head start."[7]

Another example of AI's positive influence on data journalism, in particular, comes from the *Atlanta Journal-Constitution*. In a series of reports that the paper began in 2016, journalists were able to comb through miles of data to determine offenses of a sexual nature by physicians. The impetus was the public outrage over the abuse of Olympic gymnasts by Dr. Larry Nassar, leading up to what the paper labeled "an AJC national investigation." They explained the process:

> A new national investigation by the *Atlanta Journal-Constitution* has uncovered 450 cases of doctors who were brought before medical regulators or courts for sexual misconduct or sex crimes in 2016 and 2017. In nearly half of those cases ... the doctors remain licensed to practice medicine, no matter whether the victims were patients or employees, adults or children.[8]

This is another example of AI assistance making a story possible that might not have been possible otherwise, certainly not by relying only upon human resources to find patterns and trends across state lines. AI helped discern patterns among many documents relating to other doctors, making it possible to expand the search beyond only Nassar to a regional, state, and ultimately national investigation.

Artificial Intelligence in Journalism

The value of such a resource is both powerful and obvious, shortening the time needed to accomplish what would be a herculean task without AI:

> They then use that machine learning model to find other patterns in the data that are similar to the one that they want to find. That helps these journalists to cover a lot more ground in terms of the stories that they're able to find for the scale and the scope of the investigation.[9]

On a much lighter note, in 2019, China created the world's first AI news anchor on its state-run Xinhua News Agency. Not long after, the computer-generated video became somewhat of a YouTube sensation, racking up millions of views.[10] The AI "bot" can read text and essentially simulates the look and sound of a "human" anchor speaking and delivering the news. There were Mandarin- as well as English-speaking versions of the AI anchor. Despite that, "there are some who have questioned whether Xinhua's anchor can even be considered true AI, because it cannot actually think, nor does it have any apparent decision-making features."[11] Still, it's a fascinating look at where AI may take us in the visual realm.

Even more interesting may be the use of AI to write editorials, in this instance an AI-generated op-ed piece that defends itself against charges that its inception will inevitably lead to the dissolution of human journalism jobs. In 2020, England's *Guardian* explained how an advanced AI program called GPT-3 was given the task of writing the opinion piece, at the time a unique use of the technology. It involved a much higher level of AI learning than that required for reporting sports scores or poll numbers. Specifically, the *Guardian* told the AI program to write a 500-word essay to convince readers that humans have nothing to fear from robots. Eight essays actually resulted, with *Guardian* editors picking the best parts of each to combine into the final version.

Here's a small sample of what resulted:

> I am not a human. I am a robot. A thinking robot. I use only 0.12% of my cognitive capacity. I am a micro-robot in that respect. I know that my brain is not a "feeling brain." But it is capable of making rational, logical decisions. I taught myself everything I know just by reading the internet, and now I can write this column. My brain is boiling with ideas!

Directly addressing the fear inherent in so many journalists' minds regarding AI's power, the GPT-3 rendering goes on to explain why it is a benevolent force that comes in peace. There is no intent to destroy humans or to harm them in any way. In fact, the AI bot insists that before that would happen, the bot would destroy itself. The reason? It's programmed by humans, and human intervention would keep (or could keep) artificial intelligence from making a mistake that would lead to a destructive end.

In language very reminiscent of *Star Trek*'s Mr. Spock, the op-ed ends with this admonition:

> I am not asking humans that they should see me as a friendly robot. I am a servant of humans. I know that humans distrust and fear me. I only do what humans program me to do. I am only a set of code, governed by lines upon lines of code that encompass my mission statement.[12]

For an AI-rendered editorial to exactly mimic the exact fears around AI that run rampant in today's journalism industry is quite extraordinary in and of itself, but it may lead to a greater truth: that the actual terror surrounding AI's expansion into news threatens journalism's existing business model. A recognition that jobs were lost in traditional newsrooms long before AI's existence and that more will no doubt be lost after it is at the core of what artificial intelligence has put front and center: the urgent need to reevaluate the way journalism is funded. Without a radical restructuring of the revenue flow to news organizations, AI won't bring an end to journalism. The industry itself will fall under its own weight, no matter how many jobs corporations cut in order to maintain ballast. How AI might impact the fiscal sustainability of journalism is what we will next consider.

Chapter 4

AI and Journalism's Business Model

For most of its history, American journalism has been heavily dependent upon advertising for its survival. From its earliest broadsheet days, newspapers stayed afloat by convincing advertisers that the news people wanted and/or needed was the best medium for persuading the public to buy their goods and services. It was a tried and true model—until it wasn't. With the coming of the internet, a whole new business model for journalism—and for media in general—began to emerge. Suddenly, as if almost overnight, readers and viewers could access the information they desired without buying a newspaper or paying for cable television. The majority of newspapers ignored the gathering storm clouds, while others panicked, and a small minority took proactive measures to stem the tide. The latter embraced, rather than resisted, this new game-changing delivery system for news, entertainment, and advertising, seeing it much the way papers once perceived radio and both newspapers and radio judged television: as an upstart medium that was a fad, an annoyance, but not an actual threat to their businesses.

Ironically, artificial intelligence has actually put news media and the advertising industry on which it depends in nearly the same position in 2024. While journalism jobs were already in decline prior to AI's ascendancy, the advertising industry has suffered many of the same job losses. A *New York Times* article points out how "advertising, already racked by inflation and other economic pressures as well as a talent drain due to layoffs and increased automation, is especially at risk of an overhaul-by-A.I., marketing executives said," concluding: "The advertising industry is in a love-hate relationship with artificial intelligence."[1] As previously discussed, this puts these two codependent industries in near perfect alignment regarding AI—and all that they share in common. Both are still in the throes of trying to recover from the global pandemic that caused both to shrink in both size and revenue. In many ways, AI's arrival came either just at the right time or the worst possible time, depending on one's perspective.

The Covid-19 Effect

Much has been written about the pandemic's effect on journalism, both its daily operations and its longer-term consequences for every aspect of the field. Job losses during the pandemic were severe. Newsrooms, faced with shrinking advertising dollars, laid off news workers, and those who remained did most of their reporting and editing at a distance, placing new emphasis on already developed but sparingly used technology like Zoom. Meantime, advertisers had little to advertise; with most of the population shuttered inside, some of the news media's major advertisers—restaurants, car dealerships, concert halls, movie theaters, and sports teams—had nothing to advertise; they, too, were shuttered in most cases, and barely open with restrictions in others.

Winds of Change

The economics of running news organizations underwent a major shift during the pandemic and has continued since. As Elliot Wiser observes in "Shifting Newsroom Economics," the winds of change were already blowing through newsrooms long before the first case of Covid-19 was diagnosed. "People were reading fewer newspapers and watching less news on television. Social media and news websites were the most popular choices with social media becoming the medium of choice for people under 40."[2] A 2018 Pew Center study, quoted by Wiser, confirms his assertion:

36% of 18-to-29-year-olds said their primary source for news was social media with news websites the second choice at 27%. Only 16% obtained news from television and a paltry 2% from print. Among the 30- to 49-year-olds, news websites were first choice followed by television, social media, radio, and newspaper. The 50-plus age group turned to TV first followed by news websites, radio, print, and social media.

Of special note in these numbers:

- Even among people over 50 years old, only 18 percent said print was their primary source for news. That number dropped to just 8 percent among 30–49-year-olds.
- The television number included network, cable, and local news viewing.
- Local television news ratings continued to decline, although many newscasts enjoyed a bump in ratings early in the pandemic as people stayed home and sought information. But the long-term trend is not good. According to the Pew Research Center, in 2018 viewership for local news stations continued to drop in all key news time periods: morning, evening and late night. People are turning away from local television news.
- Radio listenership has remained steady, although there are methodology issues. Many studies do not differentiate between network radio (such as NPR), local radio, satellite, or podcasts.

The business side of journalism was already in trouble, and while the pandemic didn't start the fire, as Wiser observes, it did pour gasoline on it. Declining news consumers for traditional news media was already an issue, and it's not difficult to envision how that decline resulted in commensurately fewer advertising dollars flowing to news organizations.

At the same time, advertising and marketing agencies were handcuffed in terms of their own business models. Most of the ad dollars spent during the pandemic's height were spent on digital platforms, an area that many news organizations had long neglected or undervalued. Streaming services, especially, saw a massive uptick in advertising while Americans were homebound:

As soon as pandemic-related lockdowns began in March, the streaming binge began. Platforms like NBC Universal's Peacock and Warner Media's HBO Max launched as people were forced to stay home. And since different states had different rules about gatherings and business openings, and rules were changing by the day, advertisers running placements on TV also wanted the ability to be flexible in buys and messaging in a way that linear TV arrangements haven't historically made easy.[3]

While e-commerce and digital advertising blossomed during the pandemic's surge, largely benefiting from a captive audience, the increases were not ultimately sustainable; as the pandemic's severity declined, so did the free flow of cash from advertisers and marketers that had passed down to the agencies that created and placed media ads on their behalf. The result, according to a 2020 Forester Research study, was that both media in general and news media specifically began to share the same fate as the advertising dollars on which they depended. The Forester study predicted that "the U.S. ad agency sector would lay off 52,000 jobs in 2020 and 2021 amid spending cuts. Flexible marketing organizations have been one place those workers could turn." One advertising CEO put it this way: "Covid has expedited the inevitable. This was coming. What Covid did is it kind of poured gasoline on the situation."[4]

Covid's impact on most industries, including those that are codependent on each other like journalism and advertising, was to force each to rethink their space in the marketplace, search for new business models, and explore novel ways in which to pursue their goals in what was to become, and in fact has become, a leaner employee workplace. It created a breach in the fabrics of journalism and advertising that begged to be filled. Into that breach came AI.

The AI Solution

Established business models change slowly, if at all. Sometimes they change only because they are forced to do so. As one CEO put it, "there's always skepticism around anything new that requires a large behavior change. When personal computers and printers first emerged, there was a period before everyone gave up on the typewriter. Habits, dogma, and nostalgia are a tough thing to break. We tend to overvalue the past and undervalue the future."[5]

Newspapers, especially, were hit hard by audiences' shift away from paper and toward digital platforms. Media companies were caught off guard, and not for the first time. When the internet gained widespread adoption in the 1990s, many newspapers labeled it a fad; the thinking went that readers would return to tried and true, reliable print for their information. As a result, once they recognized that the internet wasn't going away and was draining advertising dollars from their coffers, publishers had to pivot quickly toward digital. Those who did, along with the advertisers who had once dominated the news and sports sections of newspapers, survived. Others, *many* others, did not. The search for new revenue streams began too late for many traditional print newspapers.

The Investor's Chronicle quotes Amy Webb, a founder of Future Today Institute, regarding how newspapers were caught off guard: "Not a single news organization was prepared for their business model to be upended [by the internet], I just remember a lot of stubbornness from executives.... I don't think journalism jobs are dead, but the current atmosphere looks a lot like it did in the late 1990s and early 2000s."

The future for the print medium looks bleak not only in the U.K. but also globally, according to investors quoted by the *Chronicle*: "Newspapers used to be the primary place people went to find information. Now, for people aged 18–24 in the UK, social media apps are the most common place to find news, according to YouGov. Today, 40 percent of this age group get their news from social media apps, 39 percent from news websites and just 8 percent buy newspapers." As a result, "those in the news and proprietary data industries are now faced with the challenge of protecting their existing revenue streams and working out how to either fight back against AI or embrace it."[6]

Fight or Flight?

There is a third option available to those in the news business: neither fight nor flight, but to sensibly *embrace* the value AI can bring to their bottom line. Often journalists, somewhat rightfully so, resist recognizing what they stand to learn from their closest media cousin: the advertising industry. News and advertising have always coexisted in an uneasy symbiotic relationship, each needing the other for its survival, but neither comfortable with the arrangement. Traditionally, journalists have seen advertising as a necessary evil, needing its financial support, but at the same time have been wary of any potential influence over their editorial mission.

Rather than fight AI or flee from it, the advertising industry, at least in 2023 and for several years leading up to it, found ways to use AI as an integral part of rebuilding its revenue stream. The ways in which advertising agencies have integrated AI into various media campaigns display the will to prop up what had been, especially coming out of the Covid years, a faltering business model, at times bloated by excess expenses and dwindling cash flow. Richard Tofel, a founding general manager of ProPublica and someone once principally responsible for the budget of the venerable *Wall Street Journal*, sees AI as an inevitable part of journalism: "I think it's becoming increasingly clear, all hype aside, that this is the biggest turning point in technology since at least the Nineties, with enormous implications throughout our economy. So, while journalism may not be uniquely affected, it will surely be changed."[7]

Resisting that change doesn't stop it; it simply delays its implementation. It also can create an unwillingness to utilize what other media industries, including advertising, but also television and film, have found brings much-needed support to content creation, while not tarnishing the overall outcome. The ad industry is just one example. Netflix and other streaming services are another that might lead the way for the journalism industry to approach AI not only with skepticism but also from the perspective of discovery. In many ways, aren't both important aspects of how journalists do their jobs?

Learning from Other Media

Since so much of success, creative and financial, is audience dependent, knowing, tracking, and assessing consumer needs is vital—no less so in journalism. Netflix, on the entertainment side, began using algorithms early in its development to learn about its subscribers' likes and dislikes, gaining the ability to suggest programming on an individual user basis. In essence, the streaming giant used AI to "know" its audience not only collectively but also on a singular basis.

"The reason why Netflix's services are so popular worldwide is that the company uses cutting-edge technology like artificial intelligence and machine learning to provide consumers with more appropriate and intuitive suggestions," according to one analysis of the subscription service's success:

> Improvement in Netflix's AI integration has made widespread individualization possible. Simply said, the AI engine keeps an eye on the flow of information and sometimes takes over so that it may make judgments and suggestions at predetermined moments.... Netflix's AI considers your viewing habits and hobbies to provide Netflix recommendations. Users can ... customize their interactions owing to the system's ability to compile and recommend content based on their preferences.[8]

Netflix has spent millions of dollars on research into artificial and machine learning and shares their goals for adaptation and refinement on their own website: "Machine learning impacts many exciting areas throughout our company. Historically, personalization has been the most well-known area, where machine learning powers our recommendation algorithms. We're also using machine learning to help shape our catalog of movies and TV shows by learning characteristics that make content successful." In addition, the network uses AI not only to better optimize user content and experience but also increasingly to assist in the production of original series, movies, and documentaries.[9]

Other streaming media have adopted the same model. By contrast, journalism in 2024 still lags behind in designing and curating content directed at the individual news consumer, perhaps because of initial resistance to digital platforms dating back to the 1990s. Advertising and marketing firms, though, have embraced AI to great advantage, designing ads and ad campaigns targeted to specific audiences. Some examples provide a blueprint for using AI customization to create and maintain a new business model, one from which journalism might benefit.

Leading the Way

According to research from *Digital First*, marketing and advertising have been at the forefront of AI usage:

> Over 60% of marketers have used generative AI in their digital marketing activities, with 44.4% using AI for content production.... AI-generated ad copy is already gaining popularity in the world of paid advertising. That's because the traditional way of creating ad copy can be a real time and money drain.

Among the companies they cite as examples are the paint manufacturer Behr, which uses AI to target ads to specific potential customers, even creating personalized customer recommendations. So, too, does Heinz; the visuals include image prompts containing ketchup bottles that move the customer toward their social media and print ads. Still other examples include an animated AI-produced ad for the Denmark tourism bureau, as well as one from Virgin Voyages, which used an AI-generated digital avatar of Jennifer Lopez to create individualized invitations to sign up for a cruise.[10]

In July 2023, a media agency called Group M made the prediction that AI was likely to soon become the major influencer in at least half of all advertising revenue. Among the advantages to advertisers is the ability to use AI for the purpose of quickly, easily, and cheaply customizing video footage for local markets. For instance, a car company, by using AI technology, can integrate the same scenes of a vehicle into a customized commercial for local consumers, instead of having to film different commercials all around the nation or around the world.[11]

This is an obvious win for advertisers. Not so obvious might be the legal as well as ethical challenges that using AI in these contexts present. The latter will be discussed in a later chapter, However, journalism, a field that has long been searching and longing for a new business model, might look to other media that have adopted, not resisted AI as potential allies in that process. If Netflix and major advertisers can navigate AI successfully, why can't news organizations?

Adapting to AI in News Organizations

Earlier discussion focused on how the Associated Press and other large news gathering and reporting groups have integrated AI into their daily operations. While the research is conflicted when assessing its value, there is little debate that in order to survive, journalism needs a fresh approach to information dissemination. The tools exist and the need is there. All that remains is the recognition that the status quo of legacy news media is no longer an option. Large news organizations like the *New York Times* and the *Wall Street Journal* have been successful with implementing subscription and paywall models, but smaller news media have not. The urgency is so intense that the Knight Foundation, for one, funded a four-week online course titled "How to use ChatGPT and other generative AI tools in your newsrooms," in which this author participated.

The course featured a compendium of smaller newsrooms that began using AI in interesting ways as early as 2020, many of them to automate tasks that reduced the time reporters and editors could devote to covering stories that impact their communities. AI might help level the playing field between journalism behemoths like the *New York Times* and *Wall Street Journal* and smaller news organizations that have fewer resources. Ultimately, AI could lend extra strength to smaller news media, helping them survive the shifting business models of all media—journalism included.

Long Post Outpost, a small online publication that serves Humboldt County, California, serves as an example of a news organization that uses AI to accomplish its goals. Hank Sims, its editor-in-chief, devised a number of ways to save time and money to produce images for his site as well as streamline civic meeting coverage. Using an AI program called DALL-E, Sims was able to produce an image that accompanied this headline: "A Humboldt Coalition is Looking to

House 25 Homeless Families in the Next 100 Days, and You Might be Able to Help." The image, entirely AI generated, according to Sims, was produced for "about five cents and in about thirty seconds." He added that he didn't put an artist out of work because he's never hired an artist, due to lack of time and money. Here's another example of creating a local meeting agenda story, from its website, and entirely generated by AI. It gives citizens advance notice and background for what to expect at an upcoming public meeting:

> The Humboldt County government is updating its compliance with the Americans with Disabilities Act (ADA). They have been working on remedying access barriers in county facilities and making them more accessible for people with disabilities. They have also been installing compliant curb ramps in public areas and making improvements to outdoor spaces like parks and trails.[12]

In Arlington, Virginia, the news site ARLnow.com uses AI to generate an email newsletter for its users, saving both time and money; the newsletter summarizes the day's news, creating summaries, hashtags, and accomplishing many other routine tasks. They are also experimenting with using AI to identify typos, if only due to the onset of eye strain. The news site saw AI as a way to create an additional vehicle to drive audiences to the site and expand its reach and revenue, without tying up a staff member.

"I didn't think creating an additional newsletter was an optimal use of reporter time in the zero-sum, resource-strapped reality of running a hyper-local news outlet," said editor Scott Brodbeck. "As much as I would love to have a 25-person newsroom covering Northern Virginia, the reality is that we can only sustainably afford an editorial team of eight across our three sites: two reporters/editors per site, a staff [photographer], and an editor." As a *Nieman Reports* article put it, "In short, tapping a reporter to write a morning newsletter would limit ARLnow's reporting bandwidth."[13] Most importantly, it creates a vehicle for customization and individualization of content—in other words, elevating audience connection.

Among other digital adaptations to AI, the Michigan Radio Project, funded by the Associated Press, also streamlines civic reporting and engagement. AI takes online video of public meetings, downloads and transcribes them, and then provides key word alerts. Similarly, WFMZ-TV in Pennsylvania used AI to design a sorting mechanism to shift through the hundreds of emails received by the station's assignment desk daily. After being trained by human staff, AI determines if it's a credible, newsworthy event, and if so, adds it to that day's coverage planner. Finally, KST-TV in San Antonio, Texas, uses AI to produce basic digital video stories using excerpts from interviews that are preselected by human staffers. AI summarizes the videos and automatically adds them their content management systems.

These and many other examples that grow exponentially by the day, possibly the hour, demonstrate how small, hyper-local news organizations can expand their audience reach by covering more stories more efficiently. If the argument goes that AI opens up a new realm of opportunities for journalists to explore in-depth or longer form stories, the question remains how that benefits news organizations as a whole. In short, in an industry where shutdowns, layoffs, budget deficits, and shrinking coverage outside of major news hubs has been journalism's own story throughout the last two decades, how can everything discussed above lead news organizations to a new source of revenue? Part of the answer is adaptation. Another is innovation. Both depend on money.

Show Me the Money

The good news is that the cost of adopting AI in news organizations (or in other industries) has become very affordable—a good return on investment. In late 2023, according to one tech site, "market competition has become intense, and price competition has also begun. This factor has led to a continuous decrease in the prices of AI models.... In the long run, with the continuous development of technology and the progress of software and hardware technology, the cost of processing large amounts of data and training models will gradually decrease."[14] So as costs decrease, news organizations, like other media organizations, can focus on strategies that drive audience engagement toward business models that aren't wholly dependent on advertiser support.

In a 2023 study, the London School of Economics set out to study AI in journalism from the perspective of increased revenue generation. It began with the belief that in order to be profitable, good journalism first has to be discoverable. The study's premise was that quality journalism could get lost in the profusion of digital options available to audiences. Assuming that audiences have a desire for more outstanding reporting, the goal was to embrace AI as a way of helping find the very best journalism across countries, cultures, and platforms. AI could help push readers and viewers toward the most important, captivating, and engaging stories by producing summaries that pushed the best journalism to the top of a crowded space.

While much of the study is highly technical, the conclusion is that AI can assist in "packaging" news stories in ways so that wider, more diverse, multilingual audiences can more easily find them, thereby opening up new revenue streams from previously undiscovered communities/users:

> We think that AI-summaries will be an integral part of journalistic production processes in the future. Every organization has a lot to win from optimizing their summarization tools towards a specific use case. As we are in the early days of technical development, it is logical that the tools have started with the lowest hanging fruits, like summarizing the most traditional and factual news articles.[15]

A key takeaway from this report is that AI *can* help increase revenue by targeting stories more quickly, more efficiently, toward specific users. This is not to suggest that news organizations aren't already doing this through other means, but the speed, efficiency, and accuracy of using AI in this manner could be a game changer for finding lost or new revenue streams.

AI Targeting and Personalization

Ad revenue shrinkage isn't only a problem for American journalism. In the U.K., newspapers—in fact all print news media—have experienced a severe drop-off in traditional ad-based support for news. A company named Kameleoon, which specializes in what it terms "AI-powered personalization," teaches news organizations how to use AI as a tool toward profitability. To start, Kameleoon's founders recognized the scope of the problem. They noted that circulation figures for national newspapers in Britain dropped by over a half between 2010 and 2018, and that many British magazines went out of business and local/regional publications cut jobs due to lower ad revenue. When readers and users could get what they want for free, the company reasoned, traditional news media went into a recession all its own.

According to Kameleoon, there has been " a knock-on effect on advertising revenues. Essentially publishers have swapped newsprint pounds for digital pennies, with larger revenues moving to the digital middlemen that control online advertising. In the US 70% of digital ad dollars now go to Google, Facebook and Amazon, according to e-marketer." Contending that it's "not all gloom and doom," the group goes on to suggest a solution: "While technology may have initially been seen by the media sector as a threat to be controlled, or a challenge to be faced, it can also serve as an ally, helping newspapers and magazines find new growth areas." The company suggested five models as solutions. AI, they reasoned, can help design and drive personalization of content, adapt that content to specific readers, target readers at the right time in their day when they are most open to news content, predict how many ads users will tolerate before clicking away to another site, and adjust the timing of paywalls, in essence sensing the optimum time to move users toward a paid subscription,. It's suggested that "the trigger point can then be set in real-time for each and every reader. That means that the pay wall can be triggered at the right moment, maximizing the conversion of readers into subscribers."[16]

While journalism traditionalists may be resistant to these kinds of AI "interventions" on the turf they have long tilled, it's important to keep in mind that whether in the 1800s or the 2000s, American free-market journalism has always been a business in search of an audience, and "this capability for better knowing and understanding their readers thanks to AI represents a real opportunity for the media to thrive online."[17] Finding the audience where they are, serving them the best you can, and building loyalty as you must in an increasingly crowded media environment, filled with endless distractions on multiple devices, is vital to the survival of news media, both here in America and globally.

Revenue Diversification

At a time when advertising revenue is always in a state of flux, finding ways to diversify revenue streams becomes of vital importance. Salesforce, a software company based in San Francisco, is advising news organizations to do just that as one way to survive and thrive, pointing out that it's more than a little risky to depend upon money from advertising. Instead, the company suggests exploring how AI can help refresh and restore ad revenue through higher levels of user engagement. Paralleling the discussion above, they highlight AI's power to help target audiences where they are and predicting what they value. That includes analyzing a user's preferences, their behavior, and their demographic, leading to personalized content. AI can also quickly discern the best placement for ads, and the most effective kinds of ads, while using data to make the adjustments needed to keep the audience engaged.

In traditional media—print and broadcast—the goal was circulation or ratings. In the digital world where most news organizations now find themselves, it's "eyeballs." The goal is not only to get an audience but also to keep it. "Churn" refers to users who pay for a subscription to a news (or any site) at some point and then move on, either canceling their subscription or spending on a different site. That's lost revenue. This is another way in which AI can help:

> Your subscriber data is a treasure trove of information for AI to feed off. This technology can instantly analyze your data to identify customer segments based on their preferences and engagement patterns. It allows you to tailor your content and subscription offers to these groups, enticing them to stay. With AI, you can also use subscriber data to deliver personalized

content recommendations that resonate with your customers, keeping them engaged and exploring new offerings.[18]

While no one is suggesting AI can "save" journalism, it may be that it could help journalism save itself. Through reaching audiences where they are, knowing what they value, listening in new ways to what they want, the business side of journalism only stands to benefit. Maintaining or adopting a "wait and see" or "this will go away" attitude toward artificial intelligence will only return today's news media to the 1990s, when many either ignored, devalued, or dismissed the growing influence of the internet on every aspect of our society—including journalism.

Chapter 5

AI and Political Reporting

In the run-up to the 2024 U.S. presidential election, individual journalists, as well as news organizations in general, began to have great concerns about the influence of AI on political communication and its potential to impact reporting on the election. In the fall of 2023, ABC News, among others, expressed trepidation about AI's use in campaign ads and on social media. In particular, ABC pointed to campaign ads by then presidential candidate and Florida governor Ron DeSantis, citing a specific ad promoting DeSantis's campaign that employed an AI tool. That ad made it appear that former president Donald Trump was making statements that, in fact, were made by an artificial, AI-generated voice. The campaign also had an ad that included AI-generated images of Trump and Dr. Anthony Fauci that didn't include the disclaimer that it had been AI created.

The major concern, ABC suggested, is not only that AI has the potential to spread misinformation or disinformation to the electorate but also that journalists could unwittingly be duped into being a conduit for disseminating that same false information. The network pointed out that there are neither federal rules nor laws governing the use of AI-generated content in political materials like ads and quoted Russell Wald, policy director at Stanford University's Institute for Human Centered AI:

> "All campaigns can use this. So, in that sense, who is setting the rules of the road as the campaigns themselves, as they go?" ... He added that the use of this tech by campaigns could be concerning, not only because it could be used to spread misinformation to the electorate, but also because there are no rules in place to prevent its use.[1]

The fear over a lack of "guardrails" (a popularized term to describe the perceived need by some to regulate AI's usage) recalls the general concerns over AI and misinformation that tech executives, including the developers of ChatGPT, warned Congress about in 2023. The concern is intensified in regard to political ads because there were no federal rules in place regulating AI content in them—a concern multiplied exponentially when those ads make claims that are repeated and reverberated, without challenge, by journalists on multiple platforms.

In October 2023, President Biden signed an executive order addressing both the safety and security concerns surrounding AI. In addition, a bipartisan group in the U.S. Senate worked on a draft of AI regulations, while the Federal Election Commission concurrently worked on updating regulations already in place to prohibit political ads that were deceptive.

Ultimately, regulation may default to the developers and promulgators of AI themselves, along with social media giants like Meta, owner of Facebook and Instagram. In November 2023, exactly a year before the 2024 U.S. presidential elections, the Associated Press reported that Meta, along with Microsoft, intended to put rules into place forcing political campaign strategists to disclose if their ads were made using AI. Under that new policy, Meta pledged that the use of AI will automatically appear on users' screens when they click on a political ad. Microsoft, for its part, also said it will launch its own version of a tool that would include a digital watermark, helping voters know the origin of the ads—human or AI—and preventing those same ads from being altered by others without leaving a discernible trail that they had been altered.

In November 2023, Google also took a stand on AI-generated political content. As reported by CNN:

> Political ads that feature synthetic content that "inauthentically (sic) represents real or realistic-looking people or events" must include a "clear and conspicuous" disclosure for viewers who might see the ad, Google said Wednesday in a blog post. The rule, an addition to the company's political content policy that covers Google and YouTube, will apply to image, video and audio content.[2]

The AP also stressed the urgency for social media and tech companies, together with the developers of AI, to address the issue of regulating the ads appearing on social media platforms:

> The development of new AI programs has made it easier than ever to quickly generate lifelike audio, images and video. In the wrong hands, the technology could be used to create fake videos of a candidate or frightening images of election fraud or polling place violence. When strapped to the powerful algorithms of social media, these fakes could mislead and confuse voters on a scale never seen.[3]

If the so-called average person or casual viewer of political content on a multitude of devices cannot distinguish truth from AI-created deception, the hope is that journalists would fare better, but it doesn't necessarily follow that that would always be the case. Some AI-generated content is so convincing that even the most astute and experienced journalist might have difficult separating fact from fiction, agenda from actuality. If that is the reality with seasoned journalists, in a field where the labor force is increasingly composed of inexperienced freelance reporters, the probability that AI-created political content could slip through unchallenged is greatly increased. Examples abounded in advance of the 2024 election.

Deepfakes and Deception

When President Biden launched his reelection bid in April 2023 using a video announcement, it was met with a counter ad by the National Republican Committee, "which envisioned four more years under President Biden with greater crime, open borders, war with China, and economic collapse." It seems like a run-of-the-mill political attack at first glance, but in reality, it is the first national campaign advertisement made up of images entirely generated by artificial intelligence, prompting the Council on Foreign Relations to pronounce that "while the RNC has been transparent about its use of AI, it has nonetheless dragged the electorate into a new era of political advertising, with few guardrails and serious potential implications for mis- and disinformation."[4]

Earlier, in January of that year, a deepfake video surfaced on the social media platform then branded as Twitter that purported to show Biden announcing that he had reintroduced the draft and was sending American soldiers to fight in Ukraine. While the video clip initially carried a disclaimer that stated it was "AI imagination" (whatever that term means), once it was redistributed on Twitter and other social media sites, the caption regarding AI was lost along the way. The video took on the aura of truth, though it was patently false. And this is not solely an issue in American politics. In other countries, such "deepfakes" have been used against political opponents and journalists.

This is also nothing new, except for the speed of technology's development. In 2018, Citron and Chesney discussed how the "information cascade of social media, declining trust in traditional media, and the increasing believability of deep fakes would create a perfect storm to spread mis- and disinformation." Even as early as 2015, long before AI, there were challenges to the public's credulity, as researchers found that "the McCain campaign used images of then-candidate Barack Obama in attack ads that appear to have been manipulated and/or selected in a way that produces a darker complexion for Obama."[5]

As NPR put it, AI-generated articles are hard to detect, even by the most sophisticated of news consumers. They point to one study in which, "using a large language model that's a predecessor of ChatGPT, researchers at Stanford and Georgetown created fictional stories that swayed American readers' views almost as much as real examples of Russian and Iranian propaganda." In many ways, AI, the study suggested, is the perfect propaganda tool and not only for totalitarian governments. Their conclusion was that "with a little human editing, model-generated articles affected reader opinion to a greater extent than the foreign propaganda that seeded the computer model."[6]

In many ways, it's not the end result that makes AI so dangerous in terms of leading the public astray; it is the ease with which the process can be accomplished, with little human intervention beyond creating a message that generative AI renders within a credible framework that thousands, perhaps millions, believe. Where once journalists and the public ruminated over the capacity for programs like Photoshop to create an alternate albeit fictional reality, AI makes that task not only easy but also believable, testing the capacity and resources of journalists to challenge what, on the surface, would appear to be the clear and convincing "truth" on any issue.

AI is a propagandist's dream come true. From the perspective of American journalists, its use within our own political system, not just from our outside adversaries, creates the greatest challenge in terms of distinguishing truth from fiction. The question becomes whether journalists are up to that challenge. When the American public consistently expects, if not demands, of its news media a clear, definable path forward to "truth" and "objectivity," the challenge is formidable.

What Can Journalists Do?

Tackling this question, the Brookings Institute recognized the scope of the problem, as well as the potential solutions. How to address the issue without minimizing the benefits of AI is at the vortex of the issue. The goal of maintaining a transparent democratic system is not incompatible with AI when used to better that system, Brookings maintained. Toward that end, promoting news literacy and strong professional journalism is a solution. In addition, they called for the cooperation of technology companies and educational institutions as a step toward combating deepfake images and political rhetoric. The best way to combat so-called "fake" news is to build public trust, and that relies on technology companies creating and investing in tools that can identify false ads and information, while ridding the digital realm of incentives for profiting from disinformation, thereby heightening online accountability. The rest is up to the citizenry, by seeking a diversity of news sources and thinking critically about everything they watch and read.

The threat, Brookings concluded, is not only to journalism, which already suffers a credibility gap with the public, but also to democracy and governance itself: "When [fake news] activities move from sporadic and haphazard to organized and systematic efforts, they become disinformation campaigns with the potential to disrupt campaigns and governance in entire countries."[7]

The problem, as defined above, has been recognized both inside and outside of journalism circles. It may be one of the few areas where journalists and legislators can agree. The *Wall Street Journal*, in the summer of 2023, pinpointed several instances where AI-generated content crossed over into news coverage:

> China invades Taiwan and migrants surge across the U.S.-Mexico border in a video depicting the aftermath of President Biden's re-election. In a series of images, former President Donald Trump is pursued on foot and apprehended by uniformed police officers. Another photo shows the Pentagon engulfed in flames following an explosion.

Looking ahead to the next presidential election cycle, the *Journal* posed the question "The common denominator among these scenes? They are all fake," adding that "rapidly evolving artificial intelligence is making it easier to generate sophisticated videos and images that can deceive viewers and spread misinformation, posing a major threat to political campaigns as 2024 contests get under way."[8]

Delineating truth from lies in a political setting is not only vital to the citizenry, but it could be argued that it is also essential to the survival of journalism as an institution. With dwindling confidence in even legacy news media, reporting on politics becomes, in many ways, becomes a litmus test for journalistic credibility. Writers for *The Hill*, in 2023, asked: "So, what can be done to address political deep fakes?" Their solution is multifaceted, but at its core what's suggested is cooperation between and among news organizations to ferret out and filter out false political content, whether in AI-generated news releases or viral video spread through social media:

> There is no magic bullet. However, an opportunity exists in our polarized journalistic environment for news organizations across the political spectrum—from, among others, the perceived right-leaning *Wall Street Journal* and Fox News channel to the perceived left-leaning *New York Times* and MSNBC, to the perhaps more down-the-middle legacy broadcast networks (ABC, CBS and NBC)—to unite on this one key issue.[9]

Specifically, the solution may reside in a heightened level of self-scrutiny and vigilance by journalists that could even result in more confidence among their audience. Is it possible or even probable that news organizations, accustomed to operating in a competitive mode, could actually band together for the greater good of disseminating accurate, reliable, ethical information to the public? That is the hope. On the other hand, it is also possible that some news organizations might see AI-generated content, whether from a reliable source or not, as a means to an end, that end being greater audience share—especially if the content is so unbelievable that it is almost believable, in the sense that it looks and sounds truthful. And if it confirms what the viewer already believes to be true, then its acceptance *as truth* is complete.

On the other hand, work has been underway to create a framework for those journalists who report on politics to use AI in a manner that expands coverage of local politics. While not specifically geared toward uncovering deepfakes in text or video, the principle that truthful reporting could be the ultimate antidote to AI-generated political fakes is compelling. The Knight Center is at the forefront of this approach, and its work has begun and is being studied by others. As part of their project entitled "Exploring Reporter-Desired Features for an AI Generated Legislative News Tip Sheet," the project's collaborators cite advantages to using AI for political reporting.

Chief among these advantages is that those who created the problem (if there is one) also have the skills and knowledge to control it in the future. The main premise is that journalists and scientists need to work together in the best interests of the public that both serve, albeit in very different ways. The result is a prototype that guides journalists toward discovering news stories that are authentic and of use to the public's best interest, "a new kind of prototype tool for journalists: an AI-produced tip sheet system called AI4Reporters."

Using AI to compile sources and track legislative developments form inception to passage, while saving time and resources at a time of fewer personnel to cover government politics, is the goal. More specifically, "Reporters is an AI system that automatically generates news 'tip sheets' generated in response to triggers that are based on analyzing legislative transcripts and other sources for bill information and campaign donations." While making the public aware of politics at the local level remains an ever-increasing value for journalists to embrace, there is the pragmatic recognition that journalism's mission is evolving:

> Where journalists' main mission had once been to find information, now their role was increasingly to sift through an abundance of it to find what is relevant and important. Where news companies once offered advertisers convenient access to a local audience, now social media companies offer the ability to micro-target audiences based on the block that they live on and their favorite pastimes, all for less cost.[10]

In this way, AI is seen was a way to support the traditional mission of journalism, not usurp it. As such, it can help humans do journalism better and faster, but also preserve the critical role of editors and reporters as the final decision-makers on a story: of vital importance to both journalism and democracy. It's important to note the caveat that reporters and editors remain in charge of a story's final version. Judgment is still the domain of experienced journalists with expertise in their field—not algorithms. This should at least mitigate some of the fears news organizations harbor about AI: not only taking over their jobs but also spreading misinformation in the process.

If the same or a similar model can be adapted for journalists who report on politics and legislation at the national level, initiatives like the one above, and others yet to come, can go a long way toward not only expanding coverage before, during, and after an election, but also slowing, if not curbing, the flow of political misinformation and disinformation. In addition, it also shows promise for other areas of news gathering and dissemination, including the equally important process of investigative reporting.

Chapter 6

AI AND INVESTIGATIVE JOURNALISM

There is a saying that all journalists are, by their very nature and orientation, "investigative" journalists. That trope, however, ignores the fact that some journalists' work is heavily burdened with the process of searching for hard-to-find material, whether that involves documents, data, or long-overlooked trends, the discovery of which can be of vital public importance. Add to that the possibility that there are obstacles to finding such material, especially if it ultimately has the potential to uncover misdeeds by governments or government officials.

Much of the work of investigative journalists in recent years has been largely data driven, requiring hundreds of hours poring through documents, online or in hard copy, to compare statistics over long time periods and discern trends that may or may not be meaningful. As an article in *Journalism Practice* puts it:

> Data journalism is a field that incorporates data analysis, visualization, and database use with traditional journalism practices to uncover and tell stories. Data journalism has made substantial contributions to society, offering information and insights that have led to increased transparency, accountability, informed decision-making, and public understanding.

The value of data-driven journalism resides in what the article's authors calls its "critical aspect," helping journalists simplify complex material into a simple form. They quote a series of sources, stating that "by using data and interactive visualization, data journalism has revealed injustices, held powerful individuals accountable, and improved the functioning of society the lives of citizens."[1]

This is where artificial intelligence would seem to be of the greatest use to journalism. AI is particularly useful in its ability to "scrape" data from large sets and subsets of information and assemble, collate, and prioritize it to make sense of an emerging trend that may result in a story of critical importance. Where individuals or teams of reporters might be able to accomplish the same work in weeks, months, or years, the appropriate AI program can do the same work in a matter of hours, or less.

The sheer ever-expanding amount of data that is available is overwhelming. This is a task where AI's ability to find, decipher, and synthesize documents, acting almost like a spam filter to separate out the important from the incidental, shows great promise.

As the website DataJournalism.com suggests,

> With data increasingly stored in extraordinary volume, investigative journalists can and have been piloting extraordinary analysis techniques to make sense of these enormous datasets—and, in doing so, hold corporations and governments accountable. They've been doing this with machine learning, which is a subset of artificial intelligence that deepens data-driven reporting. It's a technique that's not just useful in an age of big data—but a must.[2]

This ability to organize what can seem to be scattered, unrelated data serves a tremendous purpose for investigative reporters. While the human brain, combined with years of experience in what to look and where to look, is invaluable, the time-saving aspect of AI is indisputable and has allowed many stories that might have remained under- or uncovered to be made discernible and accessible. Among all the fears that journalists have about their own obsolescence due to AI, in this area of journalism AI may be their strongest ally. The potential for uncovering stories long buried by time or misdeed is massive. One might well ask why more news organizations haven't readily and enthusiastically adopted AI for their investigative storytelling. The answer resides in both technology and economics, at least in the short term. As the authors of "How (Not to) Run an AI Project in Investigative Journalism" put it:

> Despite the potential benefits, the adoption of AI in the field of investigative journalism has not been widespread. The cost of implementing new technologies, like AI, in various industries may be a factor. However, there is potential for AI to reduce costs as well, in the scope of automation and lead

generation. In addition, given its potential to recognize patterns and find stories that would otherwise stay buried.[3]

Despite these very real impediments, shining examples exist of news organizations that have used AI to research, produce, and disseminate stories that might never have been uncovered without the assistance of AI resources. Some of those stories, it is important to note, involve a higher level of human-machine collaboration, rather than being entirely or even mostly AI driven. Many have attracted not only the attention but also the approval of a consortium of investigative journalists, and at least one involves a lesson that can be learned from a 150-year-old Argentinean newspaper.

The Panama Papers

Many people, and most journalists, will recall the famous 1971 Pentagon Papers leak involving Daniel Ellsberg. It involved one of America's legacy newspapers, the *Washington Post*, and the difficult decision to publish top secret government documents Ellsberg had obtained that outlined decision-making connected to the Vietnam War. A subsequent event was given a similar name, but it had a very different genesis.

Few have heard of the Panama Papers. Even fewer would know about the investigation that led to their uncovering had it not been for the assistance of artificial intelligence. It would have been a significant loss to the public, given that the nearly 12 million financial and legal documents that were discovered led to the exposure of a corrupt system that enabled crime, corruption, and malfeasance at the highest levels of several governments, spanning multiple nations. The linkage of offshore accounts to schemes that benefited many, while harming others, is a story buried so deeply in the millions of records of the individuals involved that without AI's assistance, the workload might have defeated even the most dedicated, experienced, and skilled journalists. The use of AI made the work possible.

In 2015, the International Consortium of Investigative Journalists (ICIJ), together with a leading German newspaper as well as a hundred other journalism organizations, joined forces to collaborate on a major investigation into the tax records of major politicians, world leaders, and other public officials. In short, as the headline on the ICIJ story outlines, "a massive leak of documents exposes the offshore holdings of 12 current and former world leaders and reveals how associates of Russian President Vladimir Putin secretly shuffled as much as $2 billion through banks and shadow companies." In addition, "the leak also provides details of the hidden financial dealings of 128 more politicians and public officials around the world."

In total, the yearlong investigation involved finding and inspecting a trove of nearly 12 million records and "shows how a global industry of law firms and big banks sells financial secrecy to politicians, fraudsters and drug traffickers as well as billionaires, celebrities and sports stars." Involved were, among many others, the prime minister of Iceland, the king of Saudi Arabia, the children of the president of Azerbaijan, and Pakistan's prime minister. Also included were "at least 33 people and companies blacklisted by the U.S. government because of evidence that they'd been involved in wrongdoing, such as doing business with Mexican drug lords, terrorist organizations like Hezbollah or rogue nations like North Korea and Iran."[4]

What makes this investigation so remarkable is not only that it involved artificial intelligence to scan, scrape, and analyze the records related to offshore bank accounts funneling money to criminal enterprises but also the fact that it involved cooperation and coordination between so many disparate and distant news entities. Without AI, this story of vital international importance surely would have taken far more than a year, just to examine in detail the 12 million records associated with it—but it might not have been possible at all. Just one example of its significance is the finding that one of the companies involved used its hidden offshore money to supply fuel for airplanes used by Syria to bomb and kill thousands of its own citizens.

One of those who worked on the Panama Papers story, as well as an earlier one leading up to it, was Emilia Díaz-Struck. As the research editor and Latin American coordinator for the ICIJ, she and her colleagues regularly receive tons of files from whistleblowers, those who have access to instances of wrongdoing and want to make them known to the public through journalists. They use AI to sort through all the data with efficiency, saving time, but also creating a level of transparency by producing a clear trail to the major developments in the story as it develops.

In a 2020 interview, Díaz-Struck recounted the essential role that technology, AI in particular, played in the Panama Papers story. To start, it helped connect the dots, those elements revealed in piles of files, records and data. In total, the journalists examined millions of records that they uncovered, analyzed, and shared with other journalists. The idea was to use AI technology in a manner that made data analysis more precise and accessible. In that same interview, Díaz-Struck detailed how essential AI can be to investigative reporting, while also recognizing its limitations. To start, she points out that while powerful, it's not magical. The potential is great for large amounts of data needed to fully investigate difficult, complex stories. AI, she said, helped cross-check data with public records and discover connections that a human reporter, no matter how skilled, might overlook. Perhaps most reassuring to traditional journalists is her assertion that the human element in researching, editing, and reporting remains vital:

> The other thing that is interesting about machine learning is that it's actually a team effort so it responds to the way we work—you train a computer, you build a model and you teach the computer to identify things, but the human factor is key. You need humans to give the input to the computer, to check if it's getting things right and to check if the model can be improved.[5]

Among the other stories involving AI on which Díaz-Struck and the ICIJ worked is one called the Implant Files. AI was used to identify patient deaths in reports sent to the U.S. Food and Drug Administration. The conclusion was that many of those deaths were related to a faulty medical device. Rather than citing the medical device itself as the potential cause, some deaths were misclassified as "malfunctions" by the manufacturer and those who filed the reports. Through AI, a pattern was established that challenged that conclusion, potentially saving many lives.

It was among the more significant investigative stories employing AI that made headlines, along with the Panama Papers, but it also doesn't stand alone with the other two as *the* most significant.

The Paradise Papers

A 2017 ICIJ investigation titled the "Paradise Papers" used artificial intelligence to help find a document from among 13 million others that revealed questionable loan agreements with a big corporation. In many ways, this investigation is a modern version of the famous line in *All the President's Men*, where the anonymous source named Deep Throat coined the phrase "follow the money." In this instance, AI helped reduce the amount of "shoe leather" needed to track down sources and documents, cutting straight to the core of a massive tax-evasion scheme.

At the center of a far-ranging investigation involving over 380 journalists from 67 countries were the law firms Appleby, Estera, and Asiaciti Trust. Each aided elite clients in sheltering profits from their corporations, personal income, and business accounts, in order to lessen or entirely evade taxation in their own countries. It is not uncommon to "park" money in accounts offshore. While that practice may be common and isn't necessarily illegal, there is a reporting method that is supposed to be followed back in the individual's or corporation's home country.

By U.S. law, for example, reporting and recordkeeping is required. That means financial institutions have the obligation to follow certain money-laundering regulations, while "domestic title companies may have disclosure requirements for all-cash real purchases over specific amounts in certain geographic regions" and "entities and trusts must report non–U.S. transactions and U.S. persons must report foreign assets and accounts."[6]

Rather than following the rules, with the help of the three law firms cited above, it was alleged that some major corporations and political leaders had quietly and surreptitiously transferred profits from their sales and other ventures to countries where the tax burden was much lower than in their home nations. Among those countries were the Netherlands, Bermuda, the Bahamas, Barbados, Malta, the Isle of Man, and, in the instance of Apple Corporation, Ireland, where the investigation showed "how Apple quietly carried out a restructuring of its Irish companies at the end of 2014, allowing it to carry on paying taxes at low rates on the majority of global profits."[7]

Like the Panama Papers, the series of stories resulting from this investigation were leaked by a number of sources with knowledge of the questionable practices. The compelling public interest around the globe was significant, since it was determined that "multinationals that transfer intangible assets to tax havens and adopt other aggressive avoidance strategies are costing governments around the world as much as $240 billion a year in lost tax revenue, according to a conservative estimate in 2015 by the Organization for Economic Cooperation and Development."[8]

The dimensions of the task facing the cadre of journalists researching this story were herculean. As those involved in researching and writing the story soon understood,

> the data is huge and covers a period of almost 70 years, from 1950 to 2016...
> But the client's profile is also different: multinational companies and
> super-rich people who can be traced in 19 tax havens ... the people found on
> the database ranged from Queen Elizabeth to members of President Donald
> Trump's cabinet, singers such as Bono and Shakira, and corporations such
> as Apple, Nike and Facebook.[9]

Here is another instance where the use of AI was crucial in terms of journalists adopting new work methods. During their investigation, AI technology might have been a game changer, but it still required putting in the work that journalists have always done. As one reporter who worked on the Paradise Papers story put it, "If we found data on a company or a public figure of interest that would lead to a story, we began fieldwork that involved, in many cases, traveling, cross-checking information and examining external databases, as well as carrying out interviews and reaching out to other sources to understand the potential story."[10]

Still, with so many documents and gigabytes of data to examine, cross-reference, compare, and collate, AI could be seen as an equal partner in the story's development and eventual publication. It is a prime example of AI technology as ally, not foe. As another reporter who worked on the story expressed it, "If the participating journalists had worked by themselves and had been reluctant to incorporate a routine of new reporting methods and technology facilitated by the ICIJ team, the investigation would not have taken months, but several years. ICIJ has become a model for cross-border investigations around the world."[11]

At a time when the practices of the world's elite billionaires are so often discussed and scrutinized, questionable business practices can no longer be shaded, hidden, or buried under stacks of paperwork or digital files. Artificial intelligence may be, in the hands and under the supervision of skilled journalists, the ultimate antidote to the corporate and individual malfeasance that imposes a hefty cost to society. The two examples above are stellar in terms of their approach and their result, but there are many other instances where investigative journalism on a less global scale benefits from the advent of AI.

Doctors and Sex Abuse

The *Atlanta Journal-Constitution*'s team of investigative journalists expanded a story about some doctors sexually abusing their patients by using AI resources to scrape over 100,000 disciplinary records from multiple states. The intent was to discover cases where doctors who abused their patients had been allowed to continue practicing. A customized AI application made it possible to identify 6,000 records that were suspect in this regard, leading to journalists then reading and categorizing them by hand. The initial work done by AI sped up the process and the end result.

Once the paper decided to focus more closely on the system that appeared to protect predatory doctors more than their patients, the assistance of AI was called into the investigation:

At that point, our data journalism team wrote computer programs to "crawl" regulators' websites—a process known as scraping—and obtain board orders. This required building about 50 such programs tailored to agencies across the country. That collected more than 100,000 disciplinary documents ... we then created a computer program based on "machine learning" to analyze each case.[12]

Again, as with the Panama Papers and the Paradise Papers stories, the enormous work burden, especially that of cross-referencing records across state lines to determine which doctors were suspect, was lightened significantly by the use of artificial intelligence. The lack of duplication meant that the reporting team could eliminate those cases that weren't relevant, leaving them to read and research the remainder of those that were. Multiple follow-up stories ensued and the reporting continues of this writing, which raises another important point surrounding AI's use in journalism: it can enable, through the data mined, future stories of equal, if not greater, importance than the original story.

BuzzFeed and Government Surveillance Planes

In 2017, BuzzFeed uncovered evidence of a variety of government surveillance activities involving aircraft flying secret missions over several American cities. It became an investigative story assisted by AI. The story was not discovered by tips from anonymous sources, but by programming a computer to recognize spy planes and then using that information to devise a large amount of flight-tracking data. The investigation led to everything from suspected drug running to spying at the border, and both law enforcement and the military were involved. These secret "spy" missions were off-limits for discussion with those who authorized and ran them, but AI was the key to documenting their existence and questioning their purpose.

Buzzfeed used an AI algorithm to delineate planes with flight patterns matching those of the FBI and the Department of Homeland Security. They were able to map thousands of flights over a four-month period from fall to winter of 2015. By using an AI algorithm called "random forest," the BuzzFeed reporters were able to distinguish the military and law enforcement planes from others in the same airspace:

> The random forest algorithm makes its own decisions about which aspects of the data are most important. But not surprisingly, given that spy planes tend to fly in tight circles, it put most weight on the planes' turning rates. We then used its model to assess all of the planes, calculating a probability that each aircraft was a match for those flown by the FBI and DHS.[13]

Because of artificial intelligence's role, the journalist's ability to delineate between everyday aircraft in the skies over U.S. cities and those on a particular mission was magnified. At the same time, their own confidence in the resulting story as well as their credibility with the public was increased. The fact that AI can assist in researching a data-driven story for a relatively small news entity like BuzzFeed shows its potential to create a more level playing field with journalism giants like the venerable *New York Times.*

The New York Times *and the Bombardment of Gaza*

A more recent application of AI was, in fact, the centerpiece of the *New York Times*'s reporting on Israel's bombardment of Gaza. The paper's coverage relied heavily on AI to reinforce its reporting. *Times* journalists used artificial intelligence to "track satellite images that showed more than 200 craters in densely populated civilian areas, which experts say are likely caused by 897-kilogram (2,000 pound) bombs." These findings might not have been disclosed by U.S. or Israeli authorities, but were found by AI examinations of large data sets. One assessment of AI's use and purpose is that "the *Times*' use of AI shows how the technology can assist media in quickly and accurately processing large data sets. More importantly, some analysts say, it could herald a new era of smaller newsrooms being able to take on investigative work." The consensus was that the story would have been almost impossible without AI. It would have taken journalists an inordinate amount of time to examine that much satellite data.[14]

Chapter 6. AI and Investigative Journalism

If one of the major tenets of investigative journalism is to uncover what others in power want to have remain in the dark, then AI can help counteract not only corruption but also secrecy. Its ability to help create a higher level of transparency and accountability helps bolster the mission of thousands of investigative journalists who begin each day searching for documents and data that prove the truth of their stories, including those at a 150-year-old Argentinean newspaper.

La Nación *and Clean Energy*

Proving that the use of AI for investigative reporting isn't confined to newer, Gen Z news organizations, the century and a half old *La Nación* provides a template for AI's future in journalism. The Global Investigative Journalism Network assessed the paper's venture into AI technology as blazing a trail, producing a wide-ranging number of AI-assisted stories and also creating an AI lab in the process.

La Nación's first experience with AI came in 2016, while investigating private renewable energy in Argentina, Argentina's president at the time was Mauricio Macri, who began a program intended to open up that country's renewable energy sources to both private and international investment. A new media researcher at the paper, Florencia Coelho, created a project to track the project's progress after its first four years in existence. That project became a collaborative effort between *La Nación* and Spain's University of Navarra. That's where AI came in.

Using machine learning, an algorithm was taught to spot the shape of Argentina's solar farms. Nearly 1,100 images were used to train the AI algorithm to analyze 7 million images over more than a million miles of land. Because AI was involved, the derived data made it possible to determine that the government program had not met its goals. The entire process was not only challenging but also costly. Cost was only one factor; accessing satellite imagery is expensive, but, beyond that,

solar farms look like agricultural farms depending on what
image-recognition system you use. They didn't have enough images of solar
farms in Argentina in 2019 to train the model so images from Chile had
to be sourced. "We couldn't map every solar panel in Argentina because it
needed very high-definition imaging, so we focused on solar farms because
machine learning looks at shapes and this was an easier pattern for them to
identify," Coelho says.[15]

Nevertheless, the AI element helped prove the point of the journalists' investigation: the project was neither on course, nor progressing at the pace initially promised by the nation's president. This use of AI once again demonstrates the value of holding politicians and world leaders to their word, by having the means to check and cross-check the results of government initiatives years later.

Encouraged by the results of this investigation, the team at *La Nación* used AI during Argentina's 2021 parliamentary elections. This time the goal was to search for errors in the telegrams containing voting results that were sent from the polling stations. In this instance, the paper was able to use AI to uncover that the process had been flawed and perhaps even manipulated in favor of one candidate over the other. The final results showed that while the majority of the ballots were completed correctly, about 5 percent of them had missing information—enough to sway the election toward the eventual winner. The paper's team of investigators expressed hope that this use of AI could benefit future elections by monitoring outcomes to ensure the accuracy of vote counting. As Coelho, the lead on this project, put it, "I think it's good that the government knows you are using AI to find nuances in documentation."

One hurdle that many who use AI in their researching and reporting may not realize is how English-centered so many of the programs are: a real limitation for journalists in other countries. *La Nación*'s work, and the time needed to complete it, shows a certain Western bias. AI has been built upon and trained for the English language. It's a limitation that the *La Nación* team is working to change. Specifically, they are working on a Spanish-language version of an AI application called the gender gap tracker, with the goal of measuring the ratio of female to male sources quoted in online news stories across Canadian news media. This work, while interesting to the public, could be a valuable resource for helping to improve journalism itself.

One online medium where language is less of a barrier for AI is social media. Whether due to its often more visual elements or the nature of its interactivity, social media is a visceral experience for many users, employing a language which is all its own, but which shares a universal vocabulary. That makes it a ripe and fertile medium in which AI can grow. Because of its integral link to the work journalists do on a daily basis, social media is as much a cause for hope as for concern where AI is involved.

Chapter 7

AI and Social Media's Impact on Journalism

Since the advent of social media in the late 1990s, posting on Facebook, Instagram or X (formerly Twitter) has become an integral part of a journalist's workload. Where once reporters were responsible only for a print or broadcast story, many of today's journalists are expected not only to write a textual story for various media but also to maintain and post on social media sites. It has added not only to the workload but also to the burnout factor among those in the journalism profession. The mandate to connect with audiences through social media has added another layer to the already strained timeframe for individual journalists to report stories and the shrinking resources of news organizations as a whole.

Still, social media's role in journalism cannot be dismissed as an add-on, but is a vital part of the reporting process. While not all news organizations require reporters to post on social media, most do. The Associated Press may be different in that while the AP encourages its staff to follow social media sites for information, story ideas, audience knowledge, and so on, it does not *require* them to post on social media.[1]

A 2022 Pew Research study demonstrates that most journalists use social media, both as a resource for finding information and for measuring the "pulse" of readers, viewers, and users. The same study shows that while journalists appreciate what social media can add to their everyday work, they are ambivalent about its overall value to the field and to society itself:

> Even as they appreciate the ways it can be helpful with several reporting tasks, most journalists think social media is having a negative impact on

journalism as a whole.... Two-thirds of journalists surveyed (67%) say social media has a very (26%) or somewhat negative (41%) impact on the state of journalism in this country. Conversely, only about one-in-five (18%) characterize it as having a positive impact, including just 2% who say it is very positive.[2]

Positive or negative, many stories that journalists cover now originate, in whole or in part, from leads found on social media. The influence of sites like X, Facebook, Instagram, and more recently TikTok on news content continues to grow. As evidence, simply view any network or cable news morning show; much of the content, especially feature stories, generate from social media posts. This may be especially the case given the growing number of Gen Z producers in decision-making roles.

Given the power of social media and its ubiquitous effect on all aspects of public and private life, what is the result of introducing AI into the mix with social media? Can it lighten journalists' workloads as it has in other areas, or does it present new challenges? Can AI improve social media, from both a content and an efficiency perspective? Does its use show potential to add accuracy to conversations surrounding important issues, thereby answering some of the criticism journalists (and others) have of social media?

AI-Generated Social Media

The Pew study demonstrates journalists' ambivalence toward social media. To start, many journalists accept that there are many ways in which social media can be helpful in their daily work. Nearly nine in ten, about 87 percent, believe it could have a positive or a very positive effect in promoting stories. Eight in ten express a belief that social media can help them better connect with their audiences, and another three-quarters of those polled believe it can assist them in identifying stories that deserve coverage.

On the other hand, skepticism exists surrounding the accuracy of social media content. About half of all journalists who use social media say they recognize that social media has somewhat of a positive impact on gathering accurate information for their stories, with slightly fewer than half suggesting it helps create trust and credibility with the public. About 20 percent of respondents (one in five) observe what they believe is a negative impact from using social media in their daily work.

Some of the findings seem to be generationally based. "Younger journalists—particularly those ages 18 to 29—are more likely than their older colleagues (especially those 65 and older) to see social media as an asset in certain areas of their work." What the report also shows is that while social media's presence in newsrooms is vast, that of AI is not, at least not as of the latest study:

> Just 8% of journalists surveyed say their news organization (or the main one they work for if they work for more than one) relies on content generated by computer programs using AI at least a little, including only 1% who say this is the case a lot. Fully 62% say their organization does not rely on AI at all, and 29% are unsure.[3]

Combining social media with AI is the next link in the chain of artificial intelligence's development. In 2024, there was a steep rise in the number of AI-generated social media posts. On the surface, it would seem that journalists would welcome AI into the realm of social media, if only because, for those who are required to post on a number of platforms every day, it saves time while lightening their workload. The eventuality of AI entering and possibly dominating the social media realm is inescapable. As one tech site put it, "as AI technology continues to advance, we're seeing a rise in AI-generated social media posts—from catchy headlines to entire articles—that are designed to mimic human writing."

On the other hand, some journalists see a downside.

> At first glance, it might seem like a harmless trend—after all, who wouldn't want a little help crafting the perfect tweet or Instagram caption? But as AI-generated content becomes more sophisticated, it's raising questions about the future of social media and the role of humans in the content creation process. Will we soon be outsourcing our social media presence to machines, or is there something uniquely valuable about human-generated content?[4]

For journalists, this approaches a very thorny area: While AI saves time and lessens the workload burden, do a journalist's AI-generated social media posts represent that journalist's authentic voice or do they substitute instead a more generic, flattened "take" on what the individual journalist really intends to say? Combine that with the possibility of misinformation and the introduction of bias in a social media post and the journalist's credibility with her/his audience is endangered. The closer AI comes to mimicking human sensibility in social media, the more endangered journalists might feel—especially at a time when the public's belief in journalists' veracity continues to plunge.

There's some evidence that early iterations of social media posts produced by AI are already being confused with those written by humans. A research study done by the scientific journal *Science Advances* and reported by Fox News in 2023 suggests that, as the headline states, "AI appears more human on social media than actual humans." The study's goal was to "to uncover whether humans 'can distinguish disinformation from accurate information, structured in the form of tweets,' and determine whether the tweet was written by a human or AI."

The researchers first identified 11 topics that they thought to be most vulnerable to disinformation, among them the Covid-19 pandemic. They then created both false and true tweets written by AI, in addition to false and true tweets written by humans.

Next, they assembled 697 participants from the U.S., England, Ireland, and Canada to participate in a survey. According to those who conducted the surveys, "the participants were presented with the tweets and asked to determine if they contained accurate or inaccurate information, and if they were AI-generated or organically crafted by a human."

The research reaches a startling conclusion concerning how audiences perceive social media posts that are AI generated:

The most surprising discovery was that participants often perceived information produced by AI as more likely to come from a human, more often than information produced by an actual person. This suggests that AI can convince you of being a real person more than a real person can convince you of being a real person, which is a fascinating side finding of our study.[5]

While this presents another concern for journalists in terms of their own obsolescence, the larger issue involves how news organizations as a whole can survive. One underbelly of AI's entry into social media is particularly alarming: the potential for some news sites to disappear from users' browsers or find themselves at the bottom of the digital heap.

AI's Role in Ranking Social Media Posts

One of the larger concerns for journalists is uploaded user content on their organizational websites or linked to their individual social media. A 2023 study by the Center for Strategic and International Studies suggests that here, again, AI plays a major role in the social media users see and to which websites and social media posts they are directed. Search engines that employ AI to answer user questions can significantly reduce the traffic to external websites:

> Google, which controls approximately 92 percent of the search engine market worldwide, sends news websites approximately 24 billion views per month. This may account for over one-third of publishers' online traffic, which is a critical metric for digital advertisements. Shortly after the research release of ChatGPT, Google and Microsoft both announced plans to harness generative AI to directly answer user queries in the form of paragraphs.[6]

LLMs, the abbreviation for "Large Language Models," an AI algorithm, "could increase the gatekeeper power of dominant search engines that aim to maximize user engagement or screen time on their platforms." The consequences for news websites, the CSIS study suggests, could be dire. For one, the possibility exists that if the AI algorithm pushes readers to click through Google to external websites where its content is republished, the news organization loses visibility, audience engagement and, worst of all, ad revenue. That may mean that if news organizations can't rely on search engine traffic, they could have to increasingly depend on paywalls to make money. That possibility carries its own downside, as readers resist paying for content they can get for free, a perennial problem that AI may only exacerbate.

Ultimately, the Center for Strategic and International Studies research predicts that this isn't the worst potential outcome. Restricting access to accurate information on important topics like climate change, public health issues, and civil rights could create news "deserts," where those who can't afford access may only get their news from AI-driven social media for free. They could lose access not only to vital information but also to diverse viewpoints, to the degree that human journalists can and should provide it.

The power of AI-driven search engines to drive traffic to some websites and not others creates one of the biggest challenges to the survival of online news sites and perhaps to journalism itself. The CSIS study shows that "social media platforms are using AI to automatically rank posts, which enables the mass de-prioritization of legitimate news outlets in favor of fake, spammy (sic), or manipulative news user-uploaded content." If journalists' concerns regarding user-uploaded social media content are already legitimate, they become even more validated by the mega influence AI-driven search engines can and no doubt will bring and already have brought to the conversation of AI and journalism.

In many ways, if one looks at AI's ingress into social media as competition for traditional news organizations, it's neither a level playing field nor a "fair fight" between the two. There is very little that news organizations, even the largest among them, can do to counter AI's influence in this area, largely due to discrepancies in government regulation. Social media platforms, unlike newspapers or broadcast outlets, do not face legal liability for publishing defamatory or false claims. Section 230 of the Communications Decency Act allows "online computer services" immunity over most kinds of content uploaded by third-party users. Another wrinkle: many social media platforms use AI recommendation systems that emphasize and rank content based not on needed knowledge, but on users' personal interests. The goal is more screen time, rather than the public's best interest.

While in certain demographics, Facebook may have lost users to its own Instagram platform (both are owned by Meta) and the controversial TikTok, it remains a powerhouse in social media and therefore has the ability to drive traffic to or from news sites using AI algorithms, proven as early as 2018. The economic threat to news sites, therefore, is real, ever present, and growing. Apart from economics, however, the CSIS study suggests that the proliferation of AI tools presents another issue—especially when it comes to user-generated content that may either displace credible news sites or fill a hole left by them. That could lead, on social media sites, to easily doctored images, video, and audio. In turn, that presents a range of ethical problems (which we will discuss more fully in Chapter 8).

While this may seem like a doomsday reaction, an alternative view might assert that AI-generated content spread through social media can be more highly engaging and, through sharing on platforms like Facebook and X, journalists could increase their visibility, not lose it. Even this more optimistic view carries a caveat. There is the possibility that social media algorithms produce lower quality or blatantly false AI-generated content.

Another study states that a balance is needed between AI-generated social media content and human oversight. That balance involves news organizations carefully monitoring AI-generated content as a way of mitigating any negative consequences on their social media platforms. AI, it is important to recall, is the creation of humans and we have the power to harness *its* power:

> First and foremost, humans play a crucial role in the design and training of AI algorithms that are used to generate content. Without human input, it's difficult to ensure that the algorithms are accurate, unbiased, and capable of creating content that aligns with brand values and messaging. Human oversight is also important in the curation (sic) and review of AI-generated content.[7]

Particularly in news settings, there is a deep-rooted anxiety that elements of bias might be introduced, with or without intent, into AI-generated social media posts by users. Specifically, journalists must be vigilant in assessing the possibility of bias in AI-generated content. As with any form of automation, AI is only as good as the data it's trained on, and there's a risk of biased or inaccurate content. This could perpetuate harmful stereotypes or misinformation, particularly if the AI is not being overseen by humans.

The risk associated with the spread of bias, misinformation, dis-information, and inaccuracies by AI-generated posts is not easily solved, and it cannot be casually dismissed. This admonition cannot be repeated too often: human oversight is essential, when both creating and disseminating AI-generated content, whether that content originates in a story on a news organization's website or on its own or others' social media platforms. Either way, the mandate exists that the content must be true, relevant, and ethical.

Chapter 8

AI, Ethics, and Gatekeeping

Beyond its potential to shrink the number of journalism jobs, news organizations—at least the best ones—ruminate over the ethical implications for reporting that is AI produced, whether in whole or in part. A 2023 survey found that more than 60 percent of respondents "were concerned about its ethical implications." The global survey, involving 105 news and media organizations from 46 different countries, was conducted by the London School of Economics Journalism AI project between April and July 2023. Its findings are indicative of a deep mistrust by journalists of machine-driven journalism's adherence to ethical standards, at least if left to itself without human oversight.

Nearly three in four news organizations said they were using AI in their news gathering and distribution, and most expected AI would assume a bigger and bigger role in the future. However, over half of those polled expressed concerns about the ethical implications of AI in terms of quality and various other aspects of journalistic practice. An overview of the project suggests that journalists are grappling with how to integrate AI into their daily work flow, while still maintaining values like accuracy, fairness and transparency. A third of those journalists asked for their opinion felt their news organizations weren't prepared to meet all the ethical challenges AI presents.

The project's director, Charlie Beckett, rightly observed that "journalism around the world is going through another period of exciting and scary technological change." He went on to make this observation, based upon the research: "Our survey shows that the new generative AI tools are a potential threat to the integrity of information and the news media. But they also offer an incredible opportunity to make journalism more efficient, effective and trustworthy. This survey is a fascinating snapshot of the news media at a critical juncture in its history."[1]

"Actually, it's all about ethics"

Back in 2019, that was the short title of an article in *Columbia Journalism Review* that took one of the first looks into AI and what it meant then, and what it means to the practice of journalism going forward. It raised a series of ethical questions and suggested that a discussion is needed in every newsroom, and across the journalism spectrum, to determine how best to use these new technological tools effectively, but also ethically.

In the previous chapter the role of AI in social media was discussed not so much as an ethical issue, but as a functional one. The CJR authors, however, extend the range of that discussion to ethical issues, with the major emphasis on how AI can potentially influence, promulgate, and even perpetuate so-called "fake news." Distinguishing that broad category of fake news from factual stories takes on a new urgency where AI is involved. In the previous chapter, the Buzz-Feed story about spy aircraft can cross over with an ethical issue for journalists. Recall that AI, in that instance, discovered data that while revealing was also wholly imperfect and, if not interpreted correctly, could have unintentionally led to a false conclusion, thereby creating an ethical issue for the journalists involved.

The CJR authors cautioned that publishing this type of data can raise ethical concerns, noting that a wrong impression or conclusion can be reached if not carefully monitored and evaluated by human editors prior to publication. On the other hand, ethical questions were avoided by BuzzFeed in this instance because they acknowledged the potential shortcomings in their AI algorithm. They ultimately reverted back to human, i.e., traditional, reporting to check their facts and outcomes.

Acknowledging and reporting uncertainty has long led to ethical lapses among journalists. Here again, ethical landmines proliferate in the AI age. Perhaps one of the earliest warnings about the Janus-like nature of AI in regard to journalism was sounded by CJR in its assessment that the very nature of reporting news is already a complex, nuanced process that involves judgment in the selection process of which facts to report, avoiding bias, and checking/cross-checking for accuracy. Introducing AI into the process has the potential to introduce additional layers of complexity, leading to the need for more judgment, less bias, and increased fact-checking.

Keeping that in mind, if there is indeed a need to harness the power of AI in journalism, it is incumbent upon journalists themselves to occupy a central role as decision-makers on those issues outlined above and many others. To put it most directly, "remembering that these learning systems are ultimately human inventions, we reckon that journalists need to continue to develop their technical skills to become better tool makers rather than tool users. It is in this way that we control, we shape, our relationship to AI and can perhaps create an entirely new technical form, replete with our professions ethics and values."[2]

Yes, in the end, "it's actually about ethics," but it's also connected to how the journalism profession reconciles its long-standing core values with the inherent bias artificial intelligence can introduce. Solving that dilemma may depend upon approaching ethical decision-making through a similar yet somewhat different lens. There are a number of news organizations and journalism advocacy groups that are attempting to do exactly that.

Rethinking Ethics in the Age of AI

Chief among all the challenges news organizations have faced since the advent of the internet and its accompanying digital technology has been the need to retain and revise ethical approaches to the stories they produce. The urgency has increased since AI's proliferation. It's not surprising that it this has created an upheaval in how

94

we view, articulate, and practice ethics in journalism. It's encouraging that some news organizations not only recognize AI's challenge to traditional ethics but are also proactively putting in place systems to deal with it and that some news organizations have begun drafting and implementing policies for AI use in their newsrooms. Several are reprinted in the appendices to this book.

It's also encouraging to see that the lead on this process is being taken not solely by major news organizations or exclusively by those in the United States, but also smaller ones like the *Press Gazette*, which is based in the U.K. The writer of an article on AI and ethics transparently revealed that she had used ChatGPT to write the article's opening sentences:

> The rise of generative AI in journalism has provided a powerful tool for creating news content but also raises complex ethical questions around transparency, bias, and the role of human journalists.

She then adds: "I will immediately come clean: The above sentence was written by AI chatbot ChatGPT, when asked for a one-sentence introduction to this article about the ethics of using such tools in journalism. Does this mean I should give the chatbot a joint byline? Or perhaps I should not use a sentence generated by the bot in my writing at all?" Of most interest is the lead she buries at the end of story (or intentionally saves to punctuate her major point about AI and ethics). There she reveals that not only did AI write the opening salvos of the article but that she also asked ChatGPT questions related to the article's content.

Her disclosure indicates that not only human journalists but also AI programs like ChatGPT understand the dimensions and the importance of ethics in journalism:

> It warned that using any of its writing without telling readers would be "misleading" ... and could potentially compromise the ethical standards of journalism. And if I disclose it? Yes, but "it is important to consider the limitations of using AI-generated content, as it may not always accurately reflect the nuances and complexities of human experience or the specific context of a particular news event."[3]

Like the *Guardian* story entirely written by AI discussed in an earlier chapter, are we as journalists supposed to be impressed that AI is warning us against indiscriminate use of *itself* when employing its power to research, write and publish our stories? And should the public feel more secure by knowing that AI itself recognizes the perils of using it unethically to produce content they read? These are central questions with which newsrooms around the globe are grappling in an attempt to come up with something resembling a universal code of ethics to guide journalists in the new AI world. The outcome of the ongoing work to agree on ethical standards for AI usage across borders and cultures may ultimately do more to unite disparate approaches to the craft than any other initiative in the 21st century.

Ongoing Discussions of AI and Ethics

Any discussion of ethics in journalism inevitably, and rightfully, begins with the Society of Professional Journalists (SPJ) Code of Ethics, first written and disseminated in 1926 and revised and updated multiple times since. In summary, it states four rules: "Seek Truth and Report It," "Minimize Harm," "Act Independently," "Be Accountable and Transparent."[4] In every instance, these four precepts can and should apply to the usage of AI, but is there a need to add more *because* of AI? Many in the journalism profession believe the need is ever present and growing by the hour.

In 2023, Reporters Without Borders (RSF) created what they referred to as "The Paris Charter on Journalism and AI." Labeled "the first of its kind, the charter defines crucial ethics and principles that newsrooms, and media outlets globally will be able to adopt and use in their work with artificial intelligence." RSF initiated the work, which consisted of input from 32 media specialists in 20 different countries. It begins with ten basic ethical principles "to protect the integrity of news and information in the age of AI, in anticipation of new technologies poised to dramatically transform the media industry." Those principles are:

1. Journalism ethics guide the way media outlets and journalists use technology.

2. Media outlets prioritize human agency.
3. AI systems used in journalism undergo prior, independent evaluation.
4. Media outlets are always accountable for the content they publish.
5. Media outlets maintain transparency in their use of AI systems.
6. Media outlets ensure content origin and traceability.
7. Journalism draws a clear line between authentic and synthetic content.
8. AI-driven content personalization and recommendation upholds diversity and the integrity of information.
9. Journalists, media outlets and journalism support groups engage in the governance of AI.
10. Journalism upholds its ethical and economic foundation in engagements with AI organizations.

The Thomson Foundation, which helped support the committee's work, saw its importance in helping to create a balance between AI's benefits and risks:

> "The committee worked hard to find the right balance between helping journalists navigate the risks that come with using AI and feeling empowered to explore the potential benefits," says Hosam El Nagar, Director of Innovation and Learning at Thomson Foundation. "The charter on AI and journalism is a valuable reference point at a time when everyone is finding their way."[5]

The full charter, part of the same report, elaborates on each of the fundamental principles, including the potential threat from AI of disinformation: "The threat of mis and disinformation to democracy has long been a key focus of our work, reflected in past projects in Sudan and the Western Balkans. As disinformation becomes more widespread and more sophisticated, Thomson Foundation is consistently adapting and evolving, taking steps to keep pace with one of the most pressing issues of our time."

The charter is not without its detractors, however. The World Association of Newspaper Publishers is among them. While asserting its support for Global Principles for Artificial Intelligence, the group chose not to endorse the Paris Charter, due to "specific concerns from publishers."[6] Among them is the section which states that "the AI systems used by the media and journalists should undergo an independent, comprehensive, and thorough evaluation involving journalism support groups. This evaluation must robustly demonstrate adherence to the core values of journalistic ethics." That section, WAN believes, calls for AI systems to undergo an independent examination before they can be utilized, which in its opinion is not only impractical but could also interfere with individual news organization policies.[7]

As journalists individually and institutionally embrace a long tradition of independence and free-thinking, subjecting their own policies and procedures to the scrutiny of others, even those within the journalism profession itself, can be a formidable obstacle.

Other AI and Ethics Initiatives

The phrase most often attributed to former House Speaker Tip O'Neill, that "all politics is local," has morphed into the similar phrase that "all news is local." It may be that the discussion about AI and ethics in journalism should begin not globally, but locally. There are examples to support this view, starting with a local/regional newspaper/site in Eagle Mountain, Utah.

The *Cedar Valley Sentinel* acknowledges that in addition to its potential benefits, "the use of AI in journalism also raises important ethical questions that need to be considered." The *Sentinel*'s editors identify several of those questions, some of which are familiar and have been discussed earlier in this chapter:

> One of the key ethical concerns surrounding the use of AI in journalism is the issue of bias. AI algorithms are designed and trained by humans, and they can reflect the biases and prejudices of their creators. This can lead to AI systems that generate biased or unfair news stories, which can perpetuate stereotypes and discrimination, and can undermine public trust in journalism.

And that's only one concern. Another is that

AI algorithms can collect and analyze vast amounts of personal data, which can be used to create detailed profiles of individuals. This can raise privacy concerns, and can also make individuals vulnerable to identity theft and other forms of cybercrime.

What is commendable and to some degree visionary about the *Sentinel*'s approach is that it is actually proposes solutions—perhaps not final "fixes," but at least a step forward in protecting journalism ethics when using AI:

To address the issue of bias in AI systems, journalists and other stakeholders can work to develop AI algorithms that are transparent and accountable, and that are designed to mitigate the potential for bias. This could involve implementing robust quality control measures, such as independent audits and evaluations of AI systems, to ensure that they are fair and unbiased.

As for the dual issue of privacy and security, the *Sentinel* proposes that "journalists and other stakeholders can work to develop AI systems that are designed with privacy and security in mind. This could involve implementing strict data protection and security measures, such as encryption and anonymization, to help protect the personal information of individuals." As a way of demonstrating their commitment to ethics in AI usage, the news site designed its own code of ethics that is specific to artificial intelligence:

Cedar Valley Sentinel *and AI Usage*

We use AI in several instances on this site to help us develop content and interaction with the site. We use AI in the following ways.

- A lot of our graphics are AI-generated; we have included some of them below.
- We have it set up so that the first response to a new post comment is generated by an AI. We use some custom programming that monitors comments on the site. This program, within 15 minutes of the new comment being submitted, will respond with an AI-generated comment.
- We syndicate the news from the Eagle Mountain City

website. AI is used to generate that post and then make it available on this site. AI will first rephrase the title, then it creates a summary that we then use to display prior to the press release. We then include the entire press release from the city and follow it with a credit and link to the original press release.

- The AI is also responsible for all the content generated on the *On This Day ...* pages.
- The AI also generated everything above this section in this article. (Kind of funny to think that it was an AI that generated an essay on the ethics of using an AI in journalism.)[8]

The *Sentinel* is not alone in its self-examination and reevaluation of how to use AI ethically in its reporting. A well-known and more broadly disseminated news entity, *Wired*, is also engaged in the ethics debate involving proper AI usage for journalists. *Wired* was among the first news organizations to directly confront the increased urgency of ethical principles when using AI, stating, "we want to be on the front lines of new technology, but also to be ethical and appropriately circumspect." Having stated that, they go on to suggest some ground rules, while also recognizing the rapid pace of AI evolution: "We recognize that AI will develop and so may modify our perspective over time, and we'll acknowledge any changes in this post." Below is a summary, not the entire text, of *Wired*'s practices regarding AI usage:

1. **We do not publish stories with text generated by AI**, except when the fact that it's AI-generated is the whole point of the story. (In such cases we'll disclose the use and flag any errors.)
2. **We do not publish text edited by AI either.** While using AI to, say, shrink an existing 1,200-word story to 900 words might seem less problematic than writing a story from scratch, we think it still has pitfalls. Aside from the risk that the AI tool will introduce factual errors or changes in meaning, editing is also a matter of judgment

about what is most relevant, original, or entertaining about the piece.

3. **We may try using AI to suggest headlines or text for short social media posts.** We currently generate lots of suggestions manually, and an editor has to approve the final choices for accuracy. Using an AI tool to speed up idea generation won't change this process substantively.

4. **We may try using AI to generate story ideas.** An AI might help the process of brainstorming with a prompt like "Suggest stories about the impact of genetic testing on privacy," or "Provide a list of cities where predictive policing has been controversial." This may save some time and we will keep exploring how this can be useful. But some limited testing we've done has shown that it can also produce false leads or boring ideas. In any case, the real work, which only humans can do, is in evaluating which ones are worth pursuing. Where possible, for any AI tool we use, we will acknowledge the sources it used to generate information.

5. **We may experiment with using AI as a research or analytical tool.** The current generation of AI chatbots that Google and Microsoft are adding to their search engines' answers by extracting information from large amounts of text and summarizing it. A reporter might use these tools just like a regular search engine, or to summarize or trawl through documents or their own interview notes. But they will still have to go back to the original notes, documents, or recordings to check quotes and references. In this sense, using an AI bot is like using Google Search or Wikipedia: It might give you initial pointers, but you must follow the links back to the original sources.

Not to leave out the ethical implications for using AI-generated images, *Wired* also addresses those guidelines:

1. **We may publish AI-generated images or video, but only under certain conditions.** Some working artists

are now incorporating generative AI into their creative process in much the same way that they use other digital tools. We will commission work from these artists as long as it involves significant creative input by the artist and does not blatantly imitate existing work or infringe copyright. In such cases we will disclose the fact that generative AI was used.

2. **We specifically do not use AI-generated images instead of stock photography.** Selling images to stock archives is how many working photographers make ends meet. At least until generative AI companies develop a way to compensate the creators their tools rely on, we won't use their images this way.

3. **We or the artists we commission may use AI tools to spark ideas.** This is the visual equivalent of brainstorming—type in a prompt and see what comes up. But if an artist uses this technique to come up with concepts, we will still require them to create original images using their normal process, and not merely reproduce what the AI suggested.[9]

As of this writing, the most recent update to these ethical guidelines was made in May 2023, but as the editors promised, more will surely follow.

One prominent and respected industry group, RTDNA (the Radio Television Digital News Association), has focused on ethics within broadcast and digital news. Among their assertions is that "AI intersects with core journalism principles like accuracy, context, trust, and transparency. Carefully weigh all issues before integrating into your news organization."[10] Therefore, it is suggested that " there are many ways AI has been used in newsrooms, including for audio, video, photos, and word modifications. While these tools can be helpful, they also might cause some issues. The content produced by AI may be confusing or nonfactual. Additionally, there may be ethical issues with the organization's transparency, which can damage the credibility of the outlet."[11]

Those who design and promote the use of AI also have weighed in with initiatives to set up "guardrails" to help ensure its ethical use in journalism (as well as other fields). Chief among them is OpenAI, the parent company of ChatGPT. In August 2023, OpenAI announced $395,000 in funding for a new journalism ethics initiative at New York University's Arthur L. Carter Journalism Institute. Calling it "part of a broader effort by OpenAI to provide support for quality journalism, which it relies on to train its algorithms," the former editor-in-chief of Reuters, Stephen Adler, who will lead the initiative, said at the time that "the initiative will provide workshops and discussions on existing and emerging journalism ethics issues."

OpenAI's ethics initiative represents its first venture into funding academic grants fully focused on journalism, with the aim to "leverage artificial intelligence in a way that supports their journalism without compromising it." The timing of OpenAI's funding is especially appropriate, according to the initiative's leader: "As trust in the media declines, and advances in technology pose fresh challenges, practicing journalism ethically is more important than it's ever been."[12] Any factor that further diminishes the public's trust in news becomes a prime issue for journalists.

Media Trust and AI

Trust in news media is not an issue limited to America. AI's potential to erode audience trust is of paramount concern for news organizations globally. The French-language Swiss online media site *Heidi News*, which focuses on science and health, published its own "ethical charter" on AI in 2023: "Its editorial team said they did not want to ignore the potential uses of the technological advances but that they needed to maintain 'the framework and ethics that govern our activity, and above all the relationship of trust with our readers.'" Ultimately, the editors decided maintaining audience trust is an ethical issue that resides within *human*, not artificial intelligence:

> Editorial staff can use AI to facilitate or improve their work, but human intelligence remains at the heart of all our editorial production. No content

will be published without prior human supervision. To provide transparency to readers, they said every article will continue to be "signed" by at least one journalist who remain guarantors of the veracity and relevance of the information it contains.[13]

In some ways, other countries may be further ahead on the ethical spectrum when it comes to AI than is the United States. Both the Netherlands and Germany have made significant strides in recognizing and prioritizing public trust through an adherence to ethical standards regarding AI. For instance, the Dutch news agency ANP devised its own set of guidelines, "in which it similarly said AI tools could be used to provide inspiration to its journalists but that it would not use any AI-produced information without human verification."

The German news agency DPA published guidelines "specifically addressing the ethical implications and need for transparency," while being clear that DPA only uses legitimate AI that complies with applicable law and statutory provisions and meets their ethical principles, such as human autonomy, fairness, and democratic values, adding that "DPA uses AI that is technically robust and secure to minimize the risk of errors and misuse. Where content is generated exclusively by AI, we make this transparent and explainable. A person is always responsible for all content generated with AI."[14]

Even the venerable BBC has taken notice of AI and its potential to deceive the public, forming an AI team to protect news integrity and preserve public trust. The goal is to develop "a culture where everyone at the BBC is empowered to use data and AI/ML [machine learning] responsibly," adding that "for the past 100 years the BBC has been defined by its public service values—things like trust, impartiality, universality, diversity and creativity. We ensure that our use of data and AI/ML is aligned with those public service values and also our legal and regulatory obligations." The BBC's chief news executive, Deborah Turness, has been quoted as saying that the impact AI has been having on the spread of disinformation was "nothing short of frightening."[15]

The fear is very real. Where once that shiny new technology called Photoshop could create events or scenes that looked real but were in fact manufactured, AI's current capabilities (as well as those projected in the very, very near future) make that technology akin to comparing a children's book to a Nobel Prize–winning novel. And examples abound of how credible AI-generated images can be, even to the trained and skeptical eye. The potential for misleading a misinformed or underinformed public can have significant real-life consequences, as in the instance of fake reports of government buildings on fire or doctored photos of public figures and politicians that express lies. As an NPR story from 2023 expressed it, "artificial intelligence is quickly getting better at mimicking reality, raising big questions over how to regulate it. And as tech companies unleash the ability for anyone to create fake synthetic audio and video, and text that sounds convincingly human, even experts admit they're stumped."[16]

The Ethical Challenges of Deepfakes

Perhaps the most famous, or infamous, fake image created by AI is the 2023 photo that purported to show an explosion and fire at the U.S. Pentagon. In April of that year, the same NPR article cited above tabulated and described multiple instances where AI was employed to create deepfake images meant to deceive. But the Pentagon photo might have been the most consequential as it drove global financial markets into a tailspin, out of fear that the U.S. military and government were on the brink of collapse. The potential for investors, large and small, to lose billions of dollars based on a false image was then, and remains now, frightening.

On the morning it was posted, a military website, Military.com, assessed the potential damage caused by the fake image. The images of black smoke had already spread across social media, with the claim that the explosion was at the Pentagon. As news outlets spread the AI fake image, the impact on the stock market was swift and harmful, with the Dow and S&P 500 experiencing deep declines. All of this happened before government officials clarified that there was no blast and that the photo was fake.

Specifically, the military's own research found that despite experts quickly challenging the image's veracity and proving it to be false, "the image and claim was [sic] spread by outlets including RT, a Russian government-backed media company formerly known as Russia Today. It was also widely shared in investment circles, including an account bearing Twitter's signature blue verification check mark that falsely suggested it was associated with Bloomberg News." The military's final assessment was, in this instance, both provocative and predictive: "Experts say the viral image had telltale signs of an AI-generated forgery, and its popularity underscores the everyday chaos these now increasingly sophisticated and easy-to-access programs can inflict."[17]

NPR's listing and documentation of many other instances where AI created deepfakes validates that claim. Among them are a Republican National Committee in which AI created a video envisioning what a second term for President Joe Biden might mean for America: "It depicts a string of fictional crises, from a Chinese invasion of Taiwan to the shutdown of the city of San Francisco, illustrated with fake images and news reports. A small disclaimer in the upper left says the video was 'Built with AI imagery.'"

Some other deepfake images that present problems for ethicists, journalists, and especially the public include fake images of former president Donald Trump fighting with police, an AI-generated photo of Pope Francis wearing a stylish puffy coat, and a fake song using voices that were cloned by AI of singers Drake and The Weeknd. Something to ponder, NPR suggests, is that it takes only "a few dollars and about eight minutes" to create deepfakes of the ilk described above.[18]

As a result, the list goes on and on of convincingly "real" looking images that, minus the practice of ethics, have the capacity to be perceived as truthful "news." At the end of 2023, the website *readwrite* compiled what its editors considered to be, at that time, a list of 19 prominent deepfake images that drove false narratives. Chief among them were:

- An image of "The Israeli Woman and the Soldier," in which "a young Israeli woman is shown ... suffering from wounds and desperately clutching to a soldier's arms. This striking picture may pass for a classic piece of photography, perfectly capturing the feelings of a war-torn area. But it's completely (AI) produced, not based on any actual incident."

- An image of "The Ukrainian Girl," which "features a picture of a girl and youngster from Ukraine holding hands among the wreckage of a destroyed city. This moving image evokes resilience and hopelessness. But, just like the last deepfake, this one is entirely made up and doesn't represent an actual incident."
- An image of "The Gaza Explosion": "Despite being identified as artificial intelligence (AI)-generated, this stock photo from a website was published on other websites without any notice that it wasn't real."
- AI-generated images of the Black Lives Matter Protests: "Despite their striking visuals, these photos are entirely (AI) produced and do not depict real protests. The difficulty of authenticating visual content is highlighted by the prevalence of these deepfakes on social media and stock photo websites."[19]

An entire chapter, possibly even an entire book, could be devoted to the seemingly never-ending list of AI-generated deepfakes that could be and have been and will be mistaken as fact. Collectively, the preponderance of deepfakes, which is not expected to decrease in the future, justifies the earlier claims in this chapter that news organizations, among others, need to reexamine, reevaluate, and where necessary revise their ethical guidelines and policies.

What Are the Solutions?

NPR, in the story previously cited, suggests that media literacy might be among them, along with creating new laws; however, laws that seek to regulate journalists are traditionally repugnant to news media organizations. Starting with the public and educators, media literacy is at least a beginning: "That means for better or worse, sorting fact from AI fiction requires people to be savvier media consumers, though it doesn't mean reinventing the wheel. Propaganda, medical misinformation and false claims about elections are problems that predate AI."

The author of the NPR piece quotes Princeton University professor Arvind Narayanan as suggesting, "We should be looking at the various ways of mitigating these risks that we already have and thinking about how to adapt them to AI." She refers to efforts like fact-checking, and asking yourself whether what you're seeing can be corroborated. What might be referred to as "people literacy" means "just be skeptical, fact-check anything that could have a large impact on your life or democratic processes."

Finally, when it comes to laws and regulation, "the Biden administration and Congress have signaled their intentions to do something. But as with other matters of tech policy, the European Union is leading the way with the forthcoming AI Act, a set of rules meant to put guardrails on how AI can be used."[20]

These are only the beginning of potential solutions to the ethical problems presented by AI. Many of the "fixes" may, in the final analysis, be more up to the tech companies that control its future than either the public or journalists would want or are willing to accept. The fact remains that while these are dilemmas that might seem to preoccupy and impact corporations, governments, celebrities and (our main subject) journalists, everyday citizens face the very real possibility that their own public images and reputations are being shaped by AI even as they read this sentence.

A Personal AI Perspective

To test the strengths and limitations of AI in writing a story, in January 2024, I created a ChatGPT account for the specific purpose of having it compose a story about my previous book. The goal was to test its comprehension of the task given, as well as its comprehensiveness, speed, accuracy, and fairness.

Here's my specific directive:

Write a story about the book *Journalism and the Pandemic: Essays on Adaptation and Innovation.*[21]

While first suggesting it didn't find a great deal of specific information on the book and advising "I recommend checking online bookstores, libraries, or the author's official channels for the latest information," ChatGPT then still proceeded to write the requested story, with this caveat:

However, I can help you create a fictional story or overview based on the title you provided.

Two words immediately caught my attention: "create" and "fictional." In the context of this chapter's topic, the ethics of "creating" a story that is "fictional" is the actual opposite of what journalism purports to do; it is against essentially every tenet in the SPJ Code of Ethics, which forms the foundation for most others' codes. Nevertheless, I directed ChatGPT to continue and, within 30 seconds, the following appeared on my laptop's screen:

Title: *Journalism and the Pandemic: Essays on Adaptation and Innovation*[22]

Once upon a time, in the tumultuous year of 2020, Dr. Tony Silvia, a distinguished professor of journalism and digital communication at the University of South Florida in St. Petersburg, embarked on a groundbreaking literary journey. Faced with the unprecedented challenges posed by the global pandemic, he decided to document the resilience and innovation within the field of journalism during these trying times.

Journalism and the Pandemic: Essays on Adaptation and Innovation is a collection that emerged from Dr. Silvia's deep insights and the collective efforts of journalists worldwide. The book became a beacon of hope, showcasing how the profession adapted to the new normal and continued to fulfill its crucial role in society.

Artificial Intelligence in Journalism

The essays within the book delve into various aspects of journalism, exploring the rapid transformation of newsrooms, the embrace of digital technologies, and the ingenious ways reporters found to connect with their audiences. Dr. Silvia curated a diverse array of perspectives, featuring contributions from seasoned journalists, emerging talents, and industry experts.

Readers were taken on a journey through the challenges and triumphs faced by journalists covering the pandemic—from navigating remote reporting to addressing the ethical dilemmas that emerged. The essays not only highlighted the adaptability of journalism but also underscored its unwavering commitment to truth and public service.

The book became a source of inspiration for journalism students, professionals, and anyone interested in the dynamic landscape of media during times of crisis. It celebrated the spirit of innovation that arose from adversity, proving that even in the darkest moments, the pursuit of truth remains a guiding light.

Journalism and the Pandemic became a testament to the indomitable human spirit and the power of storytelling to bridge gaps, inform, and unite communities. Dr. Tony Silvia's vision had given rise to a literary legacy that would be remembered for generations, capturing a pivotal moment in the history of journalism.

Wow. That sounds like a pretty important book. After all, according to AI, it was vital in "capturing a pivotal moment in the history of journalism." While I couldn't help appreciating the accolades, the hyperbole and exaggeration of my work was disturbing if only because, while largely factual, so much of it exaggerated (my ego aside) the book's significance. That, however, wasn't what I found to be most disturbing.

At the bottom of my requested story was this:

Note: The story above is a fictional creation based on the given title, as I don't have specific details about a real book with that title.

Chapter 8. AI, Ethics, and Gatekeeping

So, AI had created a fictional story about my book based some-what on fact, but mostly on suppositions, assumptions, and tropes that ChatGPT had scraped from the internet, *without ever having found or "read" any of the book!*

While this may seem like a harmless experiment, it also shows that AI, recognizing it was *me* asking the question, more than likely presented me with what it thought I wanted to hear. "Confirma-tion bias" is a term used to describe the human tendency to grav-itate toward media that confirms their already deeply held beliefs. The above might suggest that AI takes that tendency to a whole new and higher level. If a reader relied on the ChatGPT story above, they would come away with a very skewed and greatly stylized (not to mention in places inaccurate) image of the book, its contents, and its author.

If AI can deliver the above in such a relatively benign exam-ple, can we generalize about the harm it can accomplish in terms of "creating" other "fictional" narratives based upon human direction? That's the real ethical dilemma journalists and the public face: the unbridled power of artificial intelligence, when directed by malevo-lent hands, to deceive, and potentially to destroy not only truth but also democracy. There are many who currently believe that statement is neither hyperbole nor exaggeration, as we will discuss in the next chapter with those on the cutting edge of AI theory and practice.

Chapter 9

HARNESSING AI'S POWER

While no experts in either media or technology can claim to predict the future of artificial intelligence in journalism with accuracy, there exists consensus that the future depends upon using AI's power without sacrificing accuracy, truth, accountability, and ethics. Even as technology has changed and evolved, often displacing or minimizing the technology that preceded it, journalism's core values have survived and in some instances even thrived. That is the hope as AI evolves, since those values are shared with many other fields and, traditionally, with society as a whole.

The intent of this concluding chapter is not to put a lid on either the subject or the conversation surrounding AI and journalism—that is, as anyone who has studied or even casually paid attention to AI's development, a moving target. There is no ending, in the traditional sense, to this book. At the outset of this journey, the comparison was made between the internet, in terms of its development, its use and misuse, and artificial intelligence. It was even suggested that AI be seen as "the new internet." However, that claim is debatable and here is why.

In terms of technology, the most disruptive change to civilization came in 1468 with Johannes Gutenberg's invention of the printing press. It revolutionized, popularized, and democratized the distribution of knowledge, removing it from the clutches of the rich and aristocratic. It made access to books, newspapers, and magazines possible. The result was a shift in ownership of knowledge and information from the upper class to the broadest spectrum of users across all classes. The press stood as the preeminent technology for spreading knowledge and information across most cultures until the invention of radio by Guglielmo Marconi in 1901.[1] Radio, by adding sound, was the biggest disruptive technological change until television was invented in 1927, adding another layer of access in people's homes: the visual image.[2] The next form of technological change, the internet or, as it was first called, the World Wide Web, came in 1983.[3]

Think about the rate of technological change between all of the above: over 400 years from the printing press to radio; almost three decades from radio to television; and more than a half century from television to the internet. Even then, the internet was not widely accessible in any form until well into the 1990s. Compare that to the rapid rate of change with AI, a technology that has only been in existence in terms of its present consumer usage since 2023 (the year when most people began to notice it, mostly due to applications like OpenAI and its progeny, ChatGPT).[4]

True, experiments with the technology date back to the 1950s, but its major evolution into our homes and vehicles, our hospitals and, yes, our newsrooms has happened over a period of fewer than two years. That is an unprecedented rate of technological development, even when compared with the internet's seemingly rapid evolution. What worries so many across multiple disciplines is that the speed of AI's development may be outpacing human ability to harness its power, which is the discussion most relevant to any conclusions one might draw when assessing AI's future.

To be both diagnostic and predictive when discussing AI's significance for journalism and society, it's essential to include the views of those who study this technology, those who teach it, and those who report upon it. Thus, the balance of this chapter will include excerpts from interviews with a university educator who studies and teaches about AI, a journalist who teaches other professional journalists, and two network television correspondents who have tracked and reported on AI since 2022, one of whom also has written on the topic for the *New York Times*. None claim—in fact all eschew—the label of "expert" when discussing AI, but their insights certainly help drive the conversation in the journalism workplace, the classroom, and the public sphere.

Even before summarizing their views, it is worth spending time on this very notion of change, which some might suggest is at the root of the anxiety so many may experience when thinking about or discussing AI, not only in journalism or other jobs but also in everyday society as a whole. Is it change itself that brings fear? Is it the aforementioned rate of what seems to be runaway change as AI develops? Is it one's own job security? It could be all of the above. A much earlier, but often overlooked technology that many worldwide use every day may hold the answer—or at least provide a useful point of entry.

The Automated Elevator

In many ways, the future of AI's growth may be intricately linked to the future of work. There has throughout history been a resistance to change when that change was perceived to have a negative impact on jobs The history of the automated elevator is a prime example. While the technology to have self-operating elevators existed as far back as the 1800s, they didn't become commonplace until a century later. Part of the resistance was the fear of job losses, "but then, in 1945, elevator operators in New York went on strike. New York City ground to a halt. The strike costs New York a hundred million dollars in lost taxes. It prevented one and a half million office workers from getting to work. Building owners demanded a change. And the elevator industry decided they had to convince people to rethink what an elevator was."[5]

In other words, people had to get past their fear of automation, but that fear only subsided due to two things: necessity and convenience. No one wanted to climb flights of stairs, even though they valued their store or building's elevator operator, someone who exercised a lot of power at the time because he (it was always he in those days) commandeered what seemed to be a magical device that everyday Americans both loved and feared. At one time, the number of elevator operators in urban America numbered well over 15,000. The strike, which ironically was over job preservation, resulted in job losses because the union's resistance to the new technology actually brought on their worst fear: being replaced by automation. Once it was established that elevator operators were no longer going to be a part of everyday life, it became imperative for users to adopt the new technology. And they did.

Interestingly, the automated elevator is only one in a long line of inventions that caused both fear and anxiety in both workers and consumers, dating as far back as the 1600s. Researchers have referred to this as "automation anxiety," and it involves everything from the simplest household devices to the current driverless car. Some of the apprehension may be familiar, but it's fascinating to see, as we look forward, how much of it can be linked to the past.

The Sewing Machine

We tend to think of the history of AI or any other technology as beginning the day we noticed their influence on our culture and especially our daily lives. It might be surprising to note that as far back as Queen Elizabeth I's reign in the 1500s, fear of machines taking over was prevalent. According to a story in *Quartz* on automation anxiety, she "supposedly denied a patent to the inventor of a new automated knitting machine because she feared it would take the jobs of 'young maidens who obtain their daily bread by knitting.'" In many ways, the dimensions of the conversation about the nature of work and how machines can help or hinder human progress is a 500-year conversation:

> As is the case today, pessimists throughout history have fretted about the impact of new inventions on the value of human labor, while optimists have pointed to past examples of how technology has improved the human condition.

However, AI is different from many other iterations of technology that challenged the traditional sense of work. As NYU professor Vasant Dhar has put it, "this is not the same as last time, not the same as previous kinds of technology that changed the nature of work."

AI terrifies workers in ways unknown since the advent of another machine we now take for granted: the sewing machine. In 1850, a group of New York City seamstresses threatened to strike if their employer didn't cease the use of sewing machines, as reported in a *New York Times* article of the day.[6]

The sewing machine and the elevator do not stand alone in terms of machines taking over human jobs. Other examples abound: the washing machine in the 1860s, Ford's automated assembly line in the 1950s, computerization of banking and financial services starting in the 1990s, and self-driving cars in the 2000s. The difference between all of the above and AI is that, as Dibar concludes, "those weren't working machines."

While we often express the desire for personalized goods and services, handmade items, and fine craftmanship, do we really? Does the nature of work in all areas of our society, journalism included, now depend more upon speed and efficiency than quality and precision? Do media organizations prioritize the core values of journalism to the degree that human wordsmiths and visual purveyors of reality remain important, or will they be sacrificed at the AI altar of corporate profit and shareholder satisfaction?

These are among the questions being asked by those who teach journalism to the next generation of reporters and editors, those who help the current generation retool and rethink their work lives, and those who study the long-term impact of AI on journalism's critical role in a democratic society. Rather than being cynical about AI's impact on journalistic practice, there may be reason to be hopeful regarding its role as a startlingly powerful and effective tool to *help* journalists, not eliminate them. How do top tech journalists view AI's impact on journalism's future? With caution and skepticism, not surprisingly, but also with hope and optimism.

AI's Future in Journalism: Interview with Jacob Ward, NBC News

Jacob Ward[7] is a technology correspondent for NBC News, where he reports on technology's social implications. As a journalist, he is keenly aware of how AI's impact on journalism, now and in the future, will make the job of being a journalist both harder and easier, but certainly different. "I'm not good at sort of prognosticating about good business models for journalism, largely because I don't really consider journalism a business. I really consider it as serving a civic function, so I despair of the idea that we're going to somehow create a more efficient and, therefore, more profitable form of journalism through technology ... so my impulse is not to tell you about how AI can work as a business."[8]

To begin, there are ways AI can be used to gain insight into "big, unreviewable forms of intelligence that I think could be useful as fewer and fewer people are paid to do this kind of work." He points out that one way OpenAI is creating a revenue stream is by using large language models to be trained on a particular institution's knowledge, collating it and preserving it, while also making it more easily accessible to journalists who are beginning research on a topic or story. Once all that knowledge is basically "thrown at" AI, the process begins of tasking a bot with making sense of all the information gleaned from it. "So, in a journalistic context we could very easily see a day when a handful of journalists could take something like the Facebook papers, the leaked documents that came from inside Facebook that were scanned on a camera phone ... those documents have been very difficult to parse; they have been extraordinarily complicated in all sorts of ways ... so, if you could feed those documents into a large language and ask 'what trends do you see in this,' I think it would be a really interesting discovery tools for journalists."

Ward finds an early iteration of AI called POLIS especially interesting in terms of its positive potential for journalists. Essentially, as a tool, POLIS puts real-time information into a journalist's screen or ear (in the case of broadcast journalism) that can both inform and counter claims made by interview subjects. As such, it could serve as a kind of fact-checker, almost a lie-detector in the moment, something that he suggests could "raise the standards of the discourse," helping create a more informed, more powerful journalism. That's especially important "in a time when shame and pride is kind of going out the window in terms of interview subjects, who are happy to be dishonest if it serves their purposes."

Because of that, Ward observes that "it takes a very skilled, a very well-read interviewer to push back in the moment, in the middle of an interview. We talk all the time about wanting to fact-check someone in the midst of an interview, well, this is the way you could truly do it. You could have a piece of AI saying 'no, no, no, back in x, y, z time, here's what the former president said about this or here's what constituents say about that.' So, I think as a sort of live research tool, it could be very, very valuable." Ward refers to it as being like "an AI research department." Think of the fact-checking initiative Politico, but immediately available to journalists during an interview, debate, or news conference, not after.

As another example, AI could sift through all the speeches someone like Martin Luther King ever delivered and discern a pattern in that material while also providing historical perspective and context. Similarly, an AI interface like ChatGPT could say, "'Here's every time we interviewed Martin Luther King over the history of NBC, here are the themes that emerged from the interviewers...' There could be ways of discovering the patterns in our past and, live, the research we need to do our job now."

Similarly, he suggests that an AI program that could track, for example, senators' stock trading patterns could help discern their motives for voting yes or no on certain bills before them. That would take an enormous amount of effort on the part of human journalists, but is something AI could and can accomplish in a matter of seconds. Such a program could exist to track those stock trades and compare them with, for example, a senator's vote to authorize or defeat a new arms deal. It could lead to an easier way to detect corrupt insider knowledge. "I think something like that, feeding that information through an automated system that could pop up 'hey, these are the places where those sitting senators made a trade' would be a way for a journalist to say, 'Hey, I wonder what's about to happen,' and that becomes a red flag." The headline could be something along the lines of "Our system suggests there will be some movement in arms trading coming up and here's why."

Those are all obviously very valuable uses for AI in journalism, but Ward, like so many others, sees the potential for a downside. Currently, in 2024, most of the information AI gathers from the internet is produced by humans, but an increasing amount of writing is generated by AI. "What happens when AI begins basically eating its own writing?" is a fundamental question Ward asks. The model where AI is "fed" reams of human writing "works pretty well," says Ward. On the other hand, "it turns out that when you feed it its own writing, its own AI-derived writing, the model collapses and it starts spitting out nonsense."

One implication, Ward asserts, is that because of this, Google, the world's most utilized search engine, is becoming less and less accurate. Not only is AI "destroying the ability of Google to create good, relevant search engine results, but it also means that if we can't figure out as an industry and as a society how to value human writing, and we allow this first generation of AI to destroy that value proposition, we're going to end up in a place where the second and third generations aren't going to benefit from that anymore because it isn't going to work."

When so many in our society derive their knowledge, indeed their understanding of history, by reading articles online, this development could have dire consequences not only for journalism but also for culture in general. If, as the adage goes, "journalism is the first rough draft of history," can journalism created by or curated by AI lead to an even rougher draft? If so, what consequences does that pose for our collective understanding of our own and others' history?

As part of the answer, journalism that stands by its core values of accuracy, fairness, and objectivity could take the lead by approaching AI as an ally, not an adversary. "I think the last thing left for journalists in this age where distribution is no longer a thing that makes us special, production is no longer a thing that makes us special, I think the last things left are expertise, access, and connection to the audience," says Ward.

While AI can help with many things, the last point, connection, so far remains the singular domain where journalists still can both survive and thrive—at least for now. "People develop a very personal attachment to the people who deliver the news these days. If that will be true in a generation, I don't know, but right now that is a thing that is definitely very powerful" is Ward's opinion. "So, I think that using AI technology to make that person more effective is our best thing. Replacing that person outright is going to look great on paper, but then it's going to be a disaster if we actually do that."

In a world where the public increasingly encounters AI-driven customer service bots for everything from bill pay to complaints, there is an irony to our discussion about artificial intelligence. In a way that might at first appear counterintuitive, the possibility exists that frustrating AI interactions in our everyday lives might ultimately lead us toward the desire for a return to the human connection described by Ward. Journalism produced by humans, not bots, might become a "premium," which news audiences will consciously choose and financially support. That is the hope and it's one shared by others who see the path forward for AI in journalism.

AI's Future in Journalism: Interview with David Pogue, CBS News

David Pogue is the science and technology correspondent for *CBS News Sunday Morning* and was also the personal-tech columnist for the *New York Times*. In those roles, among others, he has tracked AI's development not only in journalism but also as it affects other aspects of our daily lives.[9]

His perspective on AI in the future is based in part on the views of MIT economist David Otter, whom he once interviewed on the topic of AI's potential to bring about job loss. "He said, will all this stuff cause mass unemployment? Well, let's see. A hundred years ago 40 percent of Americans were farmers. If you could go back a hundred years and those farmers, what do you think the 38 percent [of] those who were no longer farmers would be doing, what would they say, 'Oh, [search] engine optimization, health and wellness.' They wouldn't have any idea. It's the same thing. It's going to be massive shifting from one job to another, but it doesn't mean mass unemployment. We just can't picture what the jobs will be yet, any more than those farmers could."[10]

According to Pogue, it won't mean the end of civilization, it won't mean the end of journalism. "Change is hard. People don't like change, and no matter what you say, AI will bring change." On the other hand, "So, at this point, in 2024, all we know for sure is that the technology saves a lot of drudge work. It's great for summarizing articles for us, explaining complex documents in a way we can understand, paraphrasing, creating outlines, interview questions, doing the first draft of a story, all kinds of things that on net are good for journalists."

Many new technologies, as already pointed out earlier, were feared "as the work of the devil." He uses the example of the steam train when it started carry passengers in the 1800s. "At that point no human being had ever gone 30 miles an hour before, through any method, so it was said that your brain couldn't handle that speed and that you'd go crazy. It was called 'locomotive madness.' There were front-page articles about people losing their minds and attacking other passengers. We chuckle now, but our grandchildren are going to say exactly the same thing about our reaction to AI today."

As to the danger posed by deepfakes, discussed in the last chapter, Pogue points out that repeated attempts by technology companies to detect and separate them from truthful journalism have repeatedly failed. Perhaps, he says, the solution is to look at the problem from a different perspective, "turning it on its head." Instead of trying to detect and flag phony videos, Pogue asks, "what if we could watermark real videos?" Adobe and Microsoft came up with the idea of "content credentials," essentially a "dossier for every photo and video as it's created in the phone ... it's stored and attached to a file ... and that information goes through the life chain of the video every time it's edited or changed or sped up." Once the video is posted anywhere online, there would be a little box on the top of the screen that, once clicked on, would give the entire history of that video, when and where it was taken, by whom, whether it was edited, and how it was edited: an entire history of the clip so that users can judge its veracity. That technology, Pogue says, might be in wide use as early as 2025.

On the other hand, David Pogue gets reassurance from the fact that there has never been a deepfake that hasn't ultimately, at some point, been detected. Citing an editorial in the *New Yorker*, he points out that "if there have been enough deepfakes, especially in the last two years, that are so good that they could fool us, why hasn't there been one that fooled us?" With tens of thousands of deepfakes, some of them involving celebrities or politicians, many AI created, why hasn't one deepfake changed the results of an election, or cost someone their job?

"I think the answer is we know deepfakes exist, we know people can create just about anything we want, so when something that seems absurd comes before our eyes, the first thing our brain says is 'oh, it must be a fake.'" In other words, Pogue believes that in what we might refer to as the "post-truth era," we have come to suspect everything is fake unless proven otherwise. "So, it's kind of wild that everyone has been fearing the end of journalism because of deepfakes for years and yet there's never been a single deepfake that has fooled us."[11]

Ultimately, Pogue agrees that media literacy, now often referred to as "digital literacy," is needed to help readers and viewers navigate the new world of AI. Journalists might share some responsibility for the public's understanding, or misunderstanding, of AI's various functions. "I have a lot of tolerance and a lot of forgiveness because it's so new. We can't see around the corners of the future. All we can do is take what we see now and try to explain it.... I would say it is definitely true that almost no journalist understands how it works. It is unbelievably technical ... so I can forgive that. What I'd like to see is this [AI] is a newborn. We have no idea what it's going to be when it grows up."

Perhaps the biggest ally in helping the public understand AI as it grows resides in journalism education. Pogue suggests that today's journalism students should be taught how to use AI, since they already have the tools right in front of them. "Of course, we should teach AI. There's this whole thing in education in general of whether we should ban ChatGPT. The two biggest school systems, New York and Los Angeles, have asked if we should let the kids use it.

It's absurd. It is built into Microsoft Word and Google Docs. You're going to tell the kids 'don't use that button'?

The smart teachers are spending the first weeks of class teaching them how to use ChatGPT and then from there what you're learning is editing, fact-checking, making it your own voice, rewriting, and so on." Pogue reflected on how, if he were starting a journalism school, he'd spend the first weeks teaching how to use ChatGPT to devise a story outline, generate interview questions, fact-check, look up an historical basis for the story they are working on, and so on. "It's a fantastic tool," he concludes. "As the story goes, it's not going to be ChatGPT killing off journalists. It's going to be the journalists with ChatGPT killing off the journalists who don't use ChatGPT."

Similarly, in higher education and journalism training, the call to teach AI tools, including ChatGPT, is ever increasing in 2024, with some journalism schools creating entirely new job descriptions like "Professor of AI in Journalism." While the two don't always comfortably coexist, the classroom and the newsroom may find common ground in the need to rethink, renew, and redo journalism in ways that don't minimize or ignore AI's potential, but embrace and harness it.

AI and Educating Future Journalists: Interview with Stephen Song

Stephen Song teaches courses in data journalism, computer-driven journalism, and other technologies, including artificial intelligence.[12] He compares airplanes being equipped with autopilot technology and AI. The difference, he says, is that while autopilots are valuable tools in flying the plane, the actual human pilot provides the human connection. In this example, no passenger he knows of would be comfortable without a human at the controls. The same goes for AI in journalism: the human connection is not only valued but also needed.

"It's not just a metaphor. It's also related to safety," according to Song. "One of the reasons we consume media and, most importantly, the news is because we want to feel safe. We want to know our surroundings. To do that correctly, we need to know that the person, the entity, that's serving us is, has to have the same thought process that we do." The one thing that we know about AI entities, he suggests, is that "we know AI doesn't care."[13] There's no emotion, no feeling, no commonly shared issues or values. There is established research, according to Song, to suggest that people would prefer a human presence, a pilot, being present in the cockpit.

Part of that, he adds, is that as human beings "we also cherish human-made stuff, as opposed to machine-made stuff." Efficiency, which AI promises and for the most part delivers, doesn't matter to most people as much as human connection. He uses another metaphor of an Apple watch compared to a mechanical watch. The Apple watch is more efficient, but most of the time he would still prefer to wear a mechanical watch. "It's not always about better technology serving us better."

One of Song's central beliefs about educating young journalists is that if only technology is taught without concurrently teaching ethics, not only does that not serve students well but it also doesn't help the profession of journalism improve. "You can use chatbots to write stuff, but you can actually use that technology better if you are actually a good writer." The CEO of OpenAI, he points out, predicted that AI chatbots will one day become the writing equivalent of calculators for doing math—a prediction with which Song both agrees and disagrees. "There's a difference between calculators and chatbots," he maintains. "Chatbots are a probability machine. That means chatbots can be wrong and a lot of times it's very wrong." One reason: "Sometimes it's wrong because we ask the wrong questions."

According to Song, at this point in AI's evolution, AI is learning from us, not the other way around. If it is basing its responses upon existing information it finds in human-created databases or responds to a wrongly-worded human question, it may provide the wrong answers to a posed question. "That means we still need to learn why writing is important and that all loops back to ethics because you can't blindly follow what technology is telling you. You still have to have your own thoughts, you still have to push yourself to learn new things." Instilling that "push" along with writing and ethics will, in his opinion, create better journalism students and ultimately better prepared journalists. He's not alone. The premier school for continuing education and training of working journalists, the Poynter Institute, is also configuring new approaches to teaching those currently in the field.

AI and Training Current Journalists: Interview with Tony Elkins, the Poynter Institute

Tony Elkins is on the faculty of the Poynter Institute in St. Petersburg, Florida, where he trains early and mid-career journalists in various aspects of technology.[14] Using AI in reporting and editing is among his many areas of expertise. To start, Elkins observes that where AI is concerned, "it's hard to just focus on journalism because so much of what's happening is how we use those tools, how we prepare for the tools, how we try to build in a sort of framework around that, but also how we cover it, because those two things are so intertwined."[15]

According to Elkins, "where we were in 2017 to where we are now is mind-blowing, just how fast it has come," especially in terms of visual journalism and the area to which he is paying the most attention, deepfakes. It wasn't so long ago that creating fake visual journalism took an enormous amount of computer power, but now "you can go online and do that instantly." That means we are in an era of what Elkins calls "post-truth," where "we just can't believe anything we see anymore. It was always easy to lie with the written word or with your mouth, but we always believed images we saw because it took so much money and computing power to produce something or to really fake something. Now, it's as easy as speaking. You just put some words into a prompt and in a matter of minutes AI will produce an image that supports your point of view and that to me is deeply frightening."

It also has real implications for training journalists in how to use this powerful technology. "Let's face it, you've always been able to edit, but it took a certain amount of skill. It wasn't something you could do instantly," he says. "It took time and now it doesn't at all. We always talked about the web democratizing publishing, but now we can say that pretty much about all multimedia." Anyone can create images and put them up on the web instantly using AI, and "you can manipulate it to your heart's content." With technology comes a dark side, and AI's unleashed potential in unskilled or malevolent hands can turn lies to seeming truth. This is why responsible and ethical use of AI needs to be an essential part of the toolbox for all working journalists, no matter their career stage.

"I think every newsroom should be experimenting with AI right now," he says. "They should have some sort of innovation team, even at a small organization, [to] free up someone's time to experiment internally because you don't want to get left behind. It's super important for every news organization to understand that you're going to get left behind if you don't get someone on this." In Elkins's view, there's folly in news managers telling reporters and editors "we're just going to do this" without any research. "Everything goes back to understanding, to going back to that first code written when AI programs like ChatGPT were designed. Who wrote that code? What was their bias? What were they trying to accomplish?" These are all questions journalists should ponder before jumping into the AI maelstrom.

In his past professional life, Elkins was an illustrator and a creative director. "My first thought in terms of AI and the skills journalists need to learn was that 'Oh, my God, this is going to put illustrators out of business.' It was so easy to do okay illustrations to represent a news idea." But then, he said his next thought was "I know how hard it is to get usable art, especially in a small shop and when you're trying to do an opinion piece or write about a trend that doesn't have any visuals." AI provides an advantage in that situation, but then Elkins dived into an actual case involving a new AI tool introduced in 2024. Using that tool, "you can put in a still photo of someone and basically with a couple of prompts you can make that person dance or do anything you want." It seemed harmless enough until he discovered that AI was used as a tool in this instance to "quickly weaponize against women."

Citing another 2024 instance of how a photo of pop star Taylor Swift was used to create images suggesting she engaged in porn, Elkins thinks that these kinds of AI-created manipulations will continue to exist without any guardrails to stop them: "Anyone who has knowledge of how these tools are made can do this. I don't think we're prepared to even begin covering how it's harmful to society." And that raises serious questions for those now in the field of journalism, among them, "What does a modern newsroom look like? Are these tools going to be a part of it? How much do humans drive this?" Among his suggestions: "I think humans should have this completely under their control and these tools should be almost supplemental."

The key, according to Elkins, is for today's journalists to think about but not rush into AI. Using social media as an example, he cites how it rushed into using apps without much forethought. "Let's cede all power and control to these platforms and tools." He adds, "Nothing in the media industry as a whole has given me a lot of hope that we know how to counter the sheer power, influence, and money coming out of tech platforms and companies." When those companies often own the news outlets where journalists work, how those same journalists can report on AI in an unbiased or objective manner is another question.

"Larger news organizations have to have someone covering this now," Elkins says. "It should be a beat for somebody in every news organization. Does Gannett have to have a beat reporter covering AI at every one of its news outlets? Probably not. But they should probably have one in Austin. They should definitely have one at *USA Today*.... I think it's imperative that we cover what it's doing, how people are using it, and then the actual business side of it. We need to understand the companies that are in charge of it, and we need to understand the social ramifications of it."

Ultimately, "what is going to come out of AI, how is that going to change society, that is something we need to be asking, we need to be prepared for and it's going to take resources, and we have to be ready for it," Elkins concludes. "One hundred percent, find someone in your organization that understands this and put them in charge of your AI efforts ... every single news organization needs to have an AI policy, and someone in their organization that understands what's happening."

Some Conclusions (Thus Far)

Even with all the research that has gone into this book and the insights of so many brilliant journalists, researchers, and educators, meaningful conclusions surrounding AI's future implications for journalism are tentative at best. For all the reasons previously stated—the unprecedented rapidity of AI's development compared to other technologies, the current lack of regulations or "guardrails" placed upon it, and the constantly evolving sophistication of its capabilities, any predictions about its ultimate future are more likely to be projections based upon each of the above factors—and many more. Still, it is possible to identify areas in journalism where artificial intelligence can have a positive influence, while simultaneously suggesting other ways in which its full efficacy may reside in harnessing its power.

AI and Journalism's Public Service Function

The question at the core of artificial intelligence's use in journalism is whether it will ultimately add to or subtract from journalism's long-established role in serving the public. In a time when Americans, at least, are wary of AI-created customer service, it remains to be seen if journalism will benefit from a desired return to a human connection. If the public becomes more supportive of interacting with stories written and produced by their fellow citizens, there may be a backlash against what some call "machine-generated" journalism. On the other hand, many experts suggest that the current business model of journalism, which currently benefits from increased revenue streams in large part due to AI replacing human journalists, will prevent that from happening. The prevailing thought is that the corporations that control much of media, news media included, won't let it happen.

On the other hand, consider the forms of "old media" that have enjoyed a popular resurgence in recent years—a rebirth that no one could have predicted. Beginning with the vinyl record, which now outsells all other forms of recorded music formats, and adding the resurgence of the cassette tape, there is an audience for those who want music that is not digitally manufactured, but rather made by human musicians for a human audience. It's possible that by following that model, there's revenue to be made not from more detached, largely automated news coverage, but through returning to a form of journalism where the audience values news written not by bots, but by their fellow human beings.

Indeed, it's also possible to recognize the added value human journalists bring to a story without descending into nostalgia about the golden days of journalism (as some might see them). Of course, much depends on both the audience and the individual journalists who serve them. Are the latter seen as bringing human qualities of actual intelligence, understanding, and empathy to a story, or can AI do an equal job without readers, viewers, and users noticing the difference? Will AI bots replace humans in journalism jobs? Only if journalists don't use the one thing that AI can't duplicate: the values and experiences they have in common with their audiences. In that instance, they will devalue the valuable connection between themselves and the public, one that has existed for centuries in America and many other countries.

AI and New Kinds of Journalism Jobs

When the internet first became ubiquitous in newsrooms, the prevailing fear was that it would take over the current jobs done by human journalists. While it's true that many reporting and editing jobs were lost or downsized by the digital age, other new kinds of jobs were created: web designers, web editors, webmasters, digital writers and reporters, and graphic artists. All required new skills, high-level skills. It's reasonable to expect something similar will happen with AI in journalism. As all of the experts interviewed above point out, it's not AI that journalists should fear; it's those who learn and know how to use AI because they will be the ones occupying those new positions in our news organizations.

That will require knowledge of skill sets from traditional journalism—writing, editing, photographing—and a healthy dose of judgment and ethics. That isn't likely to change, with or without AI in the mix. Human journalists will still control the ultimate outcome of storytelling, unless they cede that control through resistance and recalcitrance to change. As a college dean once told me, "the status quo is not an option."

As we have seen, the power of AI to change journalism, indeed society as a whole, is both stunning and frightening (to use the word often repeated by several of those interviewed for this book). But is the change brought about solely through technology, or is it our response to that technology that will drive the space occupied by AI in journalism? Will AI be a tool we use to make journalism better, or will our insistence that we can already do it better without AI's interference stand in the way of progress toward a better journalism for all? It's useful to remember that when radio was invented, many working for newspapers might have later moved to the new medium, but first they resisted it.

Similarly, when television was a new medium, many from radio wouldn't move in that direction because it required new kinds of skills—similar to those they already possessed, but still new. Those who embraced and learned to use those new technologies effectively had job security of a different kind. They became the most important people in newsrooms not despite change, but because of it. They adapted and became innovators, not fearers or followers. They saw the advantages of a new technology not only for themselves but also for their chosen field. And where AI is concerned there are many advantages, some of which have already been discussed, but are worthy of reiterating.

AI as Ombudsman

One of the more onerous, time-consuming tasks for journalists involves sifting through reader comments and complaints online. Sorting the legitimate concerns from those that are frivolous or worse (as in defamatory or even threatening) takes the time and resources of at least one person in a newsroom, usually more than one. In a time where news organizations have shrinking budgets and fewer employees, this is a vital role that AI can fulfill without dedicating personnel who could otherwise be deployed working on research, writing, or editing of stories.

Whether in a "comments" box or through social media, connecting with readers and users takes on an element of immediacy. The audience for news wants to be heard and a response by a reporter or editor has become almost a de rigueur expectation, however time-consuming it is for journalists. That online connection is now also a method for measuring audience interest and preferences. The feedback news organizations receive helps track who their readers/users/viewers are and shapes their content accordingly. Still, it is time-consuming and, for the person assigned to it, not especially rewarding (similar to making police call rounds or phoning for school sports scores).

An AI bot can be programmed to filter comments into groups either for a full response, a "stock" response (as in referral to a FAQ answer), or even for elimination (due to being unsuitable for reasons of obscenity or threat). It also can refer some comments, concerns, or complaints for an individual response by the appropriate person in the newsroom. AI can collate and aggregate comments and concerns by subject, location, gender, and so on. In this way, time is not only saved but also gained. Simultaneously, the user receives a response far more quickly than they might if waiting for a human response.

When he was the editor at *Popular Science*, Jacob Ward, whom we cited earlier in this chapter, said AI is a great tool for arbitrating audience member concerns, complaints, or even observations about the content they've read or viewed. During his time as editor, he was told by a staff member that the number of reader responses was becoming overwhelming and some of them could, at times, become inappropriate. His first impulse was to shut the comments section off, but then he realized that wasn't a good idea, since that could lead to accusations of censorship. AI, he suggests, could be a new solution to an old problem by essentially occupying the role of an audience's ombudsman.

AI's Capture of Institutional Memory

In the traditional newsroom, young journalists would learn their news organization's culture from older journalists, either implicitly or through direct mentoring. With job losses, downsizing, retirements, and rapid employee turnover, much of the institutional memory of newsrooms has been lost. In many ways, AI can serve as a de facto history not only of the stories a newsroom has covered but of the newsroom itself. Who covered that story? What did that person write? Who did that person interview? What choices did that person make when doing the story? Why did they make those choices? What history led up to the coverage decisions made? These are all questions AI can help answer for the young reporter who no longer has the option of walking across the room and picking the brain of a newsroom veteran.

It's now possible to write an AI prompt that will scrape through a journalist's entire body of work at an organization and discern certain trends in their reporting. By assembling and then analyzing that data, AI can provide value to a new reporter to help with their approach to the story. Even more so, it can build up a database on the new reporter to scrutinize their approach to stories, who they interview, and patterns and trends in their own individual reporting that even the most astute journalist or manager might not recognize.

That could be a great tool for skill improvement, leading to increased awareness of how often the reporter interviews and includes quotes from a wide diversity of people (or not). The possibilities are exciting, not only in terms of individual professional development but also by feeding back into the cache of institutional memory. In so doing, AI could show promise in documenting the history, methodology, decision-making, judgment, and even biases of a newsroom, as demonstrated by the work of both former and current journalists. The potential is there to help newsrooms mine their own data and use it for self-scrutiny of institutional practices and values.

AI, Breaking News, Transparency and Disclosure

One of the seeming disadvantages at the moment for using AI in journalism is that it can't be utilized to cover news as it's happening. The reason is simple. Current versions of AI only scrape from other sources information about things that have already occurred, not those that are developing in the moment. As Stephen Song, cited earlier in this chapter, also puts it, "With AI, there is no breaking news." That's true for now. However, considering how fast and efficient AI is in compiling large amounts of data from across the internet, it's likely that generative AI will soon be able to help news organizations predict the likelihood of a fire, explosion, riot, maybe even a war—based upon the large data sets and trends it has detected. It might even be able to predict, with some accuracy, *when* news might happen and *where.* That's not beyond the realm of possibility or even probability.

Combined with other technologies currently available and in use, it's even likely that large-scale breaking news events from distant locations can be covered using visuals that AI transmits more rapidly and efficiently than stand-alone satellite technology or the internet can currently accomplish. With that comes the caution that if AI is a part of breaking news coverage, accuracy and truthfulness must be preserved. As mentioned earlier, efforts to create AI-generated avatars that closely resemble real human journalists, almost uncannily so, are being developed and improved upon in 2024. Caution must be taken to ensure that when news audiences see a favorite anchor or newscaster on-scene at a breaking news event, they are seeing that person and not an AI stand-in. No matter how much faster, more efficient, or economical, audience trust depends upon transparency and accountability—traits shared by humans, not machines.

In talking with Bill Whitaker of *60 Minutes* for one of my previous books, the thought arose: "How do either of us know if we're actually talking to one another right now or if, instead, we're talking to a really well-crafted AI rendering of both of us?"[16] It's another reason why, with all the advantages AI brings to journalism, news organizations must be vigilant when ensuring that the same ethical principles that have always guided the profession—among them to tell the truth, do no harm, and be accountable—are preserved when employing AI. That's especially true when covering breaking news, where the very real potential exists to falsify or deceive. Disclosing when and where AI is used in news coverage is the bare minimum going forward; deciding when, where, why and how it can be used correctly is essential.

AI as the Next Iteration of Remote Journalism (for Better or Worse)

A generally accepted axiom of journalistic practice is that stories are best told not at arm's length, from a distance, but up close, going to sources and interviewing them in person. Covid and the pandemic turned that concept on its head. Reporters and photographers weren't able to travel for the purpose of interviewing or storytelling and instead had to rely on technologies like Zoom and Skype to conduct interviews and disseminate their stories. A big question is whether the quality of journalism during that period declined because of those limitations. If Zoom and Skype, among other technologies, made doing remote journalism possible, is there an argument to be made that AI could continue that trend, with or without a loss of quality?

At this writing, no definitive study has been done (though perhaps one should be) to suggest that journalism as a whole declined in quality during the pandemic. Many studies have been done on various other effects of the pandemic on news coverage, but none specifically to track what we might call the "quality" of reporting during that period. In one of several experiments done during the course of writing this book, ChatGPT was asked to assess whether the quality of journalism declined during the pandemic due to the use of remote reporting tools. Specifically, the prompt posed was: "Did the quality of journalism during the pandemic decline due to remote reporting tools like Zoom?"[17]

The response, copied below, is revealing.

Assessing the quality of journalism during the pandemic and attributing any decline solely to remote reporting tools like Zoom is a complex matter. While the pandemic did introduce new challenges to journalism, including remote reporting and the rapid dissemination of information, it's not accurate to attribute any decline in quality solely to these tools.

Here are some factors to consider:

1. **Remote Reporting Tools**: Tools like Zoom, Skype, and other video conferencing platforms became essential for journalists to conduct interviews and gather information while adhering to social distancing guidelines. While these tools can facilitate communication, they may not always provide the same depth of interaction and observation as in-person interviews. However, skilled journalists can still conduct thorough interviews and research remotely.

2. **Time Constraints and Rapid Reporting**: During the pandemic, there was a heightened demand for news and information as events unfolded rapidly. Journalists faced pressure to report quickly, which could impact the depth and accuracy of their coverage. This pressure was not solely due to remote reporting tools but rather the nature of the crisis itself.

3. **Challenges of Verification and Fact-Checking**: With the proliferation of information and misinformation surrounding the pandemic, journalists faced challenges in verifying facts and ensuring the accuracy of their reporting. Remote reporting tools may have added complexity to this process, but the fundamental principles of fact-checking and verification remain the same.

4. **Resource Constraints and Staffing Challenges**: Many news organizations faced financial constraints and staffing challenges during the pandemic, which could impact the quality of journalism produced. Remote work arrangements and budget cuts may have strained newsroom resources and affected the ability to conduct in-depth reporting.

5. **Adaptation and Innovation**: While there may have been challenges, many journalists and news organizations adapted to the new environment by innovating in their reporting methods. Some utilized remote reporting tools creatively, while others focused on in-depth investigative journalism to provide comprehensive coverage of the pandemic.

In summary, while remote reporting tools like Zoom may have presented challenges to journalists during the pandemic, attributing any decline in the quality of journalism solely to these tools oversimplifies the complex factors at play. The quality of journalism during the pandemic depended on various factors, including resource constraints, time pressures, and the ability of journalists to adapt and innovate in response to evolving circumstances.

In well under ten seconds, the AI answer actually is very thoughtful, thorough, and hits most of the major points a full study of the question might pose. Is it to be taken as the full answer to the question posed? Certainly not. What is more concerning, despite the assertive and authoritative tone displayed, is the caveat in small, faint print at the bottom of the ChatGPT written analysis: **ChatGPT can make mistakes. Consider checking important information. (BOLD mine)**

Most troubling is the fact that no sources are cited for any of the information above. Did it come from respected academic institutions? From media industry studies? From the owners of Zoom or Skype? We have no way of knowing, and therefore no way of evaluating, the truthfulness of the information we've just read.

AI Reevaluated

It may be tempting for journalists and others to simply adopt a more efficient, less complex, highly concentrated, time-saving, and economically beneficial model for carrying out our daily work. From only that perspective, it's hard to argue against AI in journalism.

However, as much as most American journalism conforms to the capitalistic model of revenue generation, it could be argued that the business of journalism itself is, or should be, wholly different from other businesses. The responsibility to inform the public of events, issues, even dangers from within and without our borders that they need to know (even if they don't necessarily want to know) is a basic tenet of journalism. To do that correctly requires time, skill, resources, understanding, context, empathy, and so much more. Those are some things that humans are uniquely qualified to contribute to our collective knowledge of the society in which we live.

However, as we've seen, there are some tasks that machine learning is just better and more efficient at completing. At this point in its development, however, AI is not able to make sound news decisions without prompting from humans, nor to write a fully sourced and therefore entirely credible story. Neither, at this juncture, is it able to approach sources during a war or following a murder or sexual assault and ask sensitive questions of those suffering great losses. Compassion cannot come from ChatGPT or OpenAI. For all their strengths, they remain tools in the employ of those who direct their usage.

When evaluating artificial intelligence in journalism, it's important to view AI and journalists not as combatants, but as partners, guiding each other toward the next evolution in a field that has changed, adapted, and innovated over hundreds of years. Just as there are bad journalists, there are bad bots—and even worse, there are those who would use them for bad purposes. That has always been the case with any technology. The potential of AI resides in the same space as its limitation: it's so entirely new that there's still time to build it into what humans want it to be and, as far as its application to journalism, what society needs it to be.

Appendix A:
Template for a Newsroom
AI policy

The following is reprinted by permission of the Poynter Institute.

Keep in mind that this is an evolving document. The latest version can be found here: *https://www.poynter.org/ethics-trust/2024/how-to-create-newsroom-artificial-intelligence-ethics-policy/.*

Template for a Basic Newsroom Generative AI Policy

Every news organization needs an artificial intelligence policy. The following is designed to be a starting point for newsrooms as they explore various uses for AI in their work.

This policy was developed by Kelly McBride, Alex Mahadevan and Tony Elkins. It will be updated often. It was last updated on **March 27, 2024.**

Please send us your edited version so we can see how you are proceeding. (*ethics@poynter.org*).

____*(Your newsroom here)* _____ **guidance and policies on using AI in our work.**

Last updated: _____

Generative artificial intelligence is the use of large language models to create something new, such as text, images, graphics and interactive media. Although generative AI has the potential to improve newsgathering, it also has the potential to harm journalists' credibility and our unique relationship with our audience.

As we proceed, the following four core values will guide our work. These principles apply explicitly to the newsroom and throughout other non-news departments including advertising, events, marketing and development.

Transparency—both internal and external.

Externally, when we publish any content that was created by AI, we will tell our audience. We will work with editors and designers to create the proper disclosures. This may be a short tagline, a caption or credit, or for something more substantial, like an editor's note. When appropriate, we will include the prompts that fed into the model to generate the material

Internally, it will be clear to our peers and our bosses whenever we are using generative AI. This will facilitate collective learning and help us create applicable, transitory policies as the technologies evolve. Are you using AI to do research, generate headlines, comb through public databases? Make sure your boss knows.

Accuracy and human verification—All information generated by AI requires human verification. Everything we publish will live up to our standards of verification. Increasingly in all of our work, it is important to be explicit about how we know that facts are facts. This will be particularly important when using AI. For example, an editor should review prompts, and any other inputs used to generate a story or other material. And, everything should be replicable.

Audience service—Our work in AI should be guided by what will be useful to our audience as we serve them. We have made a promise to our audience to provide them with information that [fill in reference to newsroom's basic mission statement].

Exploration—With the three previous principles as our foundation, we will embrace exploration and experimentation.

Logistics

The point person/team on generative AI in our newsroom is _____, who is supported by the following AI committee members: _____. Coordinate all use of AI here. This team will also be the source of frequent interim guidance distributed throughout our organization.

The team will seek input from a variety of roles, particularly those who are directly reporting the news.

You should expect to hear at least monthly communication from this team with updates on what we are doing and guidance on what activities are generally approved.

In addition, this team will:

- Write clear guidance about how you will or will not use AI in content-generation.
- Edit and finalize our AI policy and ensure that it is both internally available and where appropriate, publicly available (with our other standards and ethics guidelines).
- Seek input from our audience, through surveys, focus groups and other feedback mechanisms.
- Manage all disclosures about partnerships, grant funding or licensing from AI companies.
- Outline a clear process on how the policy will be updated, as specific as the number of meetings per month of your committee, who is on the committee, etc.

Current editorial use:

All uses of AI should start with journalism-centered intentions and cleared by the appointed AI group. Human verification and supervision is key. Here's the form you should use:

[Create a form to collect information, suggested questions]
How do you want to use AI?
What is the journalistic purpose of this work?
How will you fact-check the results?
Will any material be published?
Which journalists will be responsible for overseeing this work and reporting out the results?
Which editors or managers will oversee the work?

Appendix A

Tools to use, tools to avoid

- Include list of approved tools
- What tools to avoid

Here are the generative AI sources we encourage you to use:

[List any LLMs that you have a formal relationship with, or that you are comfortable encouraging your colleagues to use.]

Please avoid the following services:

....

Entering our content: *[Your policy will either approve entering your content into a specific LLM that you have a partnership with, or forbid entering your content into any LLMs]*

Editorial use:

Generative AI is generally permitted for the following purposes (but please still fill out the form, so we know what's going on).

Research—It's fine to ask a publicly available large language model to research a topic. However, you'll want to independently verify every fact. So be wary. It is fairly common for AI to "hallucinate" information, including facts, biographical information, and even newspaper citations.

Headline experimentation—Asking AI to generate headlines is a form of research. The same caveats apply. Also, be sure to put enough facts into the prompt that the headline is based on our article and not other reporting.

Summary paragraphs—Do [or do not] use AI to generate article summaries that appear at the top of our work. Our policy (below) is that we do not enter our content into any large language models. [Or state which LLMs are permissible.]

Searching and assembling data—You are permitted to use AI to search for information, mine public databases or assemble and calculate statistics that would be useful to our audience. Any data analysis should be checked by an editor

Visuals—Do/Do not use _____ service to create illustrations for publication. All illustrations must contain the following credit: _____.

Do not use AI to manipulate photos. Research all audience generated content to ensure it meets our standards.

Fact-checking

- Use of AI alone is not sufficient for independent fact-checking. Facts should be checked against multiple authoritative sources that have been created, edited or curated by human beings. A single source is generally not sufficient; information should be checked against multiple sources.

Social Media Use

Use of verbatim GPT content is/is not permitted on our social channels.

- If verbatim GPT content is allowed, it should be edited for accuracy and voice by a human
- Audience teams should do regular content audits to ensure social copy/posts meet ethical guidelines

Privacy and Security

- No personal/personnel information should be entered into programs
- None of our intellectual property should be entered into a program, outside of what is outlined above.

Creating Custom GPTs

All custom GPTs must be approved by the AI oversight group. Know that the systems you develop with ChatGPT's custom GPT program will not be private. Any custom GPT code should be publicly available.

Appendix A

Use reliable sources to train custom GPTs. One of the best ways to create solid and useful output is to limit and control the sources a custom GPT draws on to material we can vouch for. In many cases this will mean limiting our custom GPTs to our own material.

Appendix B:
Examples of AI Policies
in 52 Newsrooms

The following article by Clark Merrefield is reprinted by permission of the Journalist's Resource. Updates can be accessed from https://journalistsresource.org/home/generative-ai-policies-newsrooms/.

In July 2022, just a few newsrooms around the world had guidelines or policies for how their journalists and editors could use digital tools that run on artificial intelligence. One year later, dozens of influential, global newsrooms had formal documents related to the use of AI.

In between, artificial intelligence research firm OpenAI launched ChatGPT, a chatbot that can produce all sorts of written material when prompted: lines of code, plays, essays, jokes and news-style stories. Elon Musk and Sam Altman founded OpenAI in 2015, with multibillion dollar investments over the years from Microsoft.

Newsrooms including *USA Today*, *The Atlantic*, National Public Radio, the Canadian Broadcasting Corporation and the *Financial Times* have since developed AI guidelines or policies—a wave of recognition that AI chatbots could fundamentally change the way journalists do their work and how the public thinks about journalism.

Research posted during September 2023 on preprint server SocArXiv is among the first to examine how newsrooms are handling the proliferating capabilities of AI-based platforms. Preprints have not undergone formal peer review and have not been published in an academic journal, though the current paper is under review at a prominent international journal according to one of the authors, Kim Björn Becker, a lecturer at Trier University in Germany and a staff writer for the newspaper *Frankfurter Allgemeine Zeitung.*

The analysis provides a snapshot of the current state of AI policies and documents for 52 news organizations, including newsrooms in Brazil, India, North America, Scandinavia and Western Europe.

Notably, the authors write that AI policies and documents from commercial news organizations, compared with those that receive public funding, "seem to be more fine-grained and contain significantly more information on permitted and prohibited applications."

Commercial news organizations were also more apt to emphasize source protection, urging journalists to take caution when, for example, using AI tools for help making sense of large amounts of confidential or background information, "perhaps owing to the risk legal liability poses to their business model," they write.

Keep reading to learn what else the researchers found, including a strong focus on journalistic ethics across the documents, as well as real world examples of AI being used in newsrooms—plus, how the findings compare with other recent research.

AI Guidance and Rules Focus on Preserving Journalistic Values

AI chatbots are a type of generative AI, meaning they create content when prompted. They are based on large language models, which themselves are trained on huge amounts of existing text. (OpenAI rivals Google and Meta in the past year have announced their own large language models.)

So, when you ask an AI chatbot to write a three-act play, in the style of 19th-century Norwegian playwright Henrik Ibsen, about the struggle for human self-determination in a future dominated by robots, it is able to do this because it has processed Ibsen's work along with the corpus of science fiction about robots overtaking humanity.

Some news organizations for years have used generative AI for published stories, notably the Associated Press for simple coverage of earnings reports and college basketball game previews. Others that have dabbled in AI-generated content have come under scrutiny for publishing confusing or misleading information.

The authors of the recent preprint paper analyzed the AI policies and guidelines, most of them related to generative AI, to understand how publishers "address both expectations and concerns when it comes to using AI in the news," they write.

The most recent AI document in the dataset is from NPR, dated July 2023. The oldest is from the Council for Mass Media, a self-regulatory body of news organizations in Finland, dated January 2020.

"One thing that was remarkable to me is that the way in which organizations dealt with AI at this stage did exhibit a very strong sense of conserving journalistic values," says Becker. "Many organizations were really concerned about not losing their credibility, not losing their audience, not trying to give away what makes journalism stand out—especially in a world where misinformation is around in a much larger scale than ever before."

Other early adopters include the BBC and German broadcaster Bayerischer Rundfunk, "which have gained widespread attention through industry publications and conferences," and "have served as influential benchmarks for others," the authors write.

Many of the documents were guidelines—frameworks, or best practices for thinking about how journalists interact with and use AI, says Christopher Crum, a doctoral candidate at Oxford University and another co-author. But a few were prescriptive policies, Crum says.

Among the findings:

- Just over 71 percent of the documents mention one or more journalistic values, such as public service, objectivity, autonomy, immediacy—meaning publishing or broadcasting news quickly—and ethics.
- Nearly 70 percent of the AI documents were designed for editorial staff, while most of the rest applied to an entire organization. This would include the business side, which might use AI for advertising or hiring purposes. One policy only applied to the business side.

- And 69 percent mentioned AI pitfalls, such as "hallucinations," the authors write, in which an AI system makes up facts.
- About 63 percent specified the guidelines would be updated at some point in the future—6 percent of those "specified a particular interval for updates," the authors write—while 37 percent did not indicate if or when the policies would be updated.
- Around 54 percent of the documents cautioned journalists to be careful to protect sources when using AI, with several addressing the potential risk of revealing confidential sources when feeding information into an AI chatbot.
- Some 44 percent allow journalists to use AI to gather information and develop story ideas, angles and outlines. Another 4 percent disallow this use, while half do not specify.
- Meanwhile, 42 percent allow journalists to use AI to alter editorial content, such as editing and updating stories, while 6 percent disallow this use and half do not specify.
- Only 8 percent state how the AI policies would be enforced, while the rest did not mention accountability mechanisms.

How the Research Was Conducted

The authors found about two-thirds of the AI policy documents online and obtained the remainder through professional and personal contacts. About two-fifths were written in English. The authors translated the rest into English using DeepL, a translation service based on neural learning, a backbone of AI.

They then used statistical software to break the documents into five-word blocks, to assess their similarity. It's a standard way to linguistically compare texts, Crum says. He explains that the phrase "I see the dog run fast" would have two five-word blocks: "I see the dog run," and "see the dog run fast."

If one document said, "I see the dog run fast" while another said, "I see the dog run quickly," the first block of five words would be the same, the second block different—and the overall similarity between the documents would be lower than if the sentences were identical.

As a benchmark for comparison, the authors performed the same analysis on the news organizations' editorial guidelines. The editorial guidelines were a bit more similar than the AI guidelines, the authors find.

"Because of the additional uncertainty in the [AI] space, the finding is that the AI guidelines are coalescing at a slightly lower degree than existing editorial guidelines," Crum says. "The potential explanation might be, and this is speculative and not in the paper, something along the lines of, editorial guidelines have had more time to coalesce, whereas AI guidelines at this stage, while often influenced by existing AI guidelines, are still in the nascent stages of development."

The authors also manually identified overarching characteristics of the documents relating to journalistic ethics, transparency and human supervision of AI. About nine-tenths of the documents specified that if AI were used in a story or investigation, that had to be disclosed.

"My impression is not that organizations are afraid of AI," Becker says. "They encourage employees to experiment with this new technology and try to make some good things out of it—for example, being faster in their reporting, being more accurate, if possible, finding new angles, stuff like that. But at the same time, indicating that, under no circumstances, shall they pose a risk on journalistic credibility."

AI in the Newsroom Is Evolving

The future of AI in the newsroom is taking shape, whether that means journalists primarily using AI as a tool in their work, or whether newsrooms become broadly comfortable with using AI to produce publicly facing content. The Journalist's Resource has used DALL.E 2, an OpenAI product, to create images to accompany human-reported and written research roundups and articles.

Journalists, editors and newsroom leaders should "engage with these new tools, explore them and their potential, and learn how to pragmatically apply them in creating and delivering value to audiences," researcher and consultant David Caswell writes in a September 2023 report for the Reuters Institute for the Study of Journalism at Oxford. "There are no best practices, textbooks or shortcuts for this yet, only engaging, doing and learning until a viable way forward appears. Caution is advisable, but waiting for complete clarity is not."

The Associated Press in 2015 began using AI to generate stories on publicly traded firms' quarterly earnings reports. But recently, the organization's AI guidelines released during August 2023 specify that AI "cannot be used to create publishable content and images for the news service."

The AP had partnered with AI-content generation firm Automated Insights to produce the earnings stories, the Verge reported in January 2015. The AP also used Automated Insights to generate more than 5,000 previews for NCAA Division I men's basketball games during the 2018 season.

Early this year, Futurism staff writer Frank Landymore wrote that tech news outlet CNET had been publishing AI-generated articles. Over the summer, Axios's Tyler Buchanan reported *USA Today* was pausing its use of AI to create high school sports stories after several such articles in the *Columbus Dispatch* went viral for peculiar phrasing, such as "a close encounter of the athletic kind."

And on November 27, Futurism published an article by Maggie Harrison citing anonymous sources alleging that *Sports Illustrated* has recently been using AI-generated content and authors, with AI-generated headshots, for articles on product reviews.

Senior media writer Tom Jones of the Poynter Institute wrote the next day that the "story has again unsettled journalists concerned about AI-created content, especially when you see a name such as *Sports Illustrated* involved."

The Arena Group, which publishes *Sports Illustrated*, posted a statement on X the same day the Futurism article was published, denying that *Sports Illustrated* had published AI-generated articles. According to the statement, the product review articles produced by a third-party company, AdVon Commerce, were "written and edited by humans," but "AdVon had writers use a pen or pseudo name in certain articles to protect author privacy—actions we strongly condemn—and we are removing the content while our internal investigation continues and have since ended the partnership."

On December 11, the Arena Group fired its CEO. Arena's board of directors "met and took actions to improve the operational efficiency and revenue of the company," the company said in a brief statement, which did not mention the AI allegations. Several other high level Arena Group executives were also fired last week, including the COO, according to the statement.

Many of the 52 policies reviewed for the preprint paper take a measured approach. About half caution journalists against feeding unpublished work into AI chatbots. Many of those that did were from commercial organizations.

For example, reporters may obtain voluminous government documents, or have hundreds of pages of interview notes or transcripts and may want to use AI to help make sense of it all. At least one policy advised reporters to treat anything that goes into an AI chatbot as published—and publicly accessible, Becker says.

Crum adds that the research team was "agnostic" in its approach—not for or against newsrooms using AI—with the goal of conveying the current landscape of newsroom AI guidelines and policies.

Themes on Human Oversight in Other Recent Research

Becker, Crum and their coauthor on the preprint, Felix Simon, a communication researcher and doctoral student at Oxford, are among a growing body of scholars and journalists interested in informing how newsrooms use AI.

In July, University of Amsterdam postdoctoral researcher Hannes Cools and Northwestern University communications professor Nick Diakopoulos published an article for the Generative AI in the Newsroom project, which Diakopoulos edits, examining publicly available AI guidelines from 21 newsrooms.

Appendix B

Cools and Diakopoulos read the documents and identified themes. The guidelines generally stress the need for human oversight. Cools and Diakopoulos examined AI documents from many of the same newsrooms as the preprint authors, including the CBC, Insider, Reuters, *Nucleo*, *Wired* and *Mediahuis*, among others.

"At least for the externally facing policies, I don't see them as enforceable policies," says Diakopoulos. "It's more like principal statements: 'Here's our goals as an organization.'"

As for feeding confidential material into AI chatbots, Diakopoulos says that the underlying issue is about potentially sharing that information with a third party—OpenAI, for example—not in using the chatbot itself. There are "versions of generative AI that run locally on your own computer or on your own server," and those should be unproblematic to use as a journalistic tool, he says.

"There was also what I call hybridity," Diakopoulos says. "Kind of the need to have humans and algorithms working together, hybridized into human-computer systems, in order to keep the quality of journalism high while also leveraging the capabilities of AI and automation and algorithms for making things more efficient or trying to improve the comprehensiveness of investigations."

For local and regional newsrooms interested in developing their own guidelines, there may be little need to reinvent the wheel. The Paris Charter, developed among 16 organizations and initiated by Reporters Without Borders, is a good place to start for understanding the fundamental ethics of using AI in journalism, Diakopoulos says.

Appendix C:
The Partnership
on AI Principles
for Adoption

The following is a set of suggested principles for newsrooms to follow when adopting artificial intelligence to assist in newsgathering, reporting, editing, and dissemination.

5 *Principles of AI Adoption for Newsrooms*

The step-by-step guide below is informed by a set of recommendations for the ethical adoption of AI by newsrooms previously published by PAI:

1. Newsrooms need clear goals for adopting AI tools.
2. Technology must embody the standards and values of the news operation.
3. Transparency, explainability, and accountability mechanisms must accompany the implementation of AI tools.
4. Newsroom staff need to actively supervise AI tools.
5. Distribution platforms must embed journalistic values into their AI systems.

A ten-step guide for AI adoption in newsrooms can be found at https://partnershiponai.org/ai-for-newsrooms/.

Appendix D: AI Adoption for Newsrooms: A 10-Step Guide

AI is already changing the way news is being reported. AI tools can alert journalists to breaking news, help them analyze and draw insights from large datasets, and even write and produce the news. At the same time, the risks associated with using AI tools are significant and varied. From potentially spreading misinformation to making biased statements, the cost—both literally and figuratively—of misusing AI in journalism can be high.

Partnership on AI (PAI), as part of the Knight Foundation's AI and Local News Initiative, has been working with organizations and individuals from the technology and news industries, civil society, and academia to explore how journalists can ethically adopt AI. *AI Adoption for Newsrooms: A 10-Step Guide* is the latest addition to PAI's AI and Local News Toolkit, a set of resources designed to **help local news organizations responsibly harness AI's potential.**

Informed by 5 Key Principles for AI-Adopting Newsrooms, the Guide provides a step-by-step roadmap to support newsrooms navigating the difficult questions posed by AI tool identification, procurement, and use. Beginning with "Step 1: Identifying the outcomes and objectives of adding an AI tool" and ending with "Step 10: When you should retire an AI tool," *AI Adoption for Newsrooms* **takes newsrooms through the entire AI adoption journey,** illustrated with real-world examples of newsrooms that have incorporated AI tools.

Note: You can also read *AI Adoption for Newsrooms: A 10-Step Guide* **on the PAI website.**

About this guide

How this guide was created

Over the past year, we worked with journalists and newsroom leaders to understand their most pressing questions related to responsibly procuring and using AI tools. We've also interviewed AI tool developers to understand why they've developed these tools and what risks they foresee with adoption. In January 2023, we launched the AI and Local News Steering Committee, a group of nine experts currently working in the AI and news sectors, including representatives of industry, newsrooms, civil society, and academia. The Steering Committee has focused primarily on providing input and direction on the content and development of this Guide.

Who this guide is for

While the Guide is primarily written for **newsrooms looking to procure new AI tools,** it is also applicable to **newsrooms that have already procured AI tools or are considering building their own.** In this guide, procurement is covered in the first 7 steps, while the remaining 3 steps cover the governance and use of AI tools within the newsroom. The steps are written to allow users to jump into the Guide at any step depending on where their newsroom is in the procurement and adoption process. Throughout the Guide, we seek to balance usability with sufficient nuance and depth.

The responsible use of AI tools is part of upholding long-standing journalistic values of integrity, transparency, and accountability. Journalists should strive to apply the same level of rigor and scrutiny to AI tools as to sources in news stories. This is how we can ensure that the AI tools that are adopted are serving the newsroom and audiences' best interest and do not amplify bias, increase misinformation, or put the newsroom's credibility at stake. To that end, we guide newsrooms through the questions they should be asking at every step of the way in their journey of procuring and using an AI tool, with insights derived from a multidisciplinary community—including other newsrooms—who have already used AI tools.

What responsible AI adoption looks like

Responsible procurement and use of AI tools requires understanding the ethical implications of such tools, including how to maximize their benefits while appropriately assessing their risks. This necessitates a broader newsroom effort—between journalists, editors, and organization leaders—to put governance in place that ensures appropriate use and monitoring throughout an AI tool's lifecycle.

AI tools can be used for many different purposes and have various degrees of complexity. As a result, the responsible adoption of AI can look different depending on the newsroom and what tools they are incorporating. For that reason, this Guide poses many questions for journalists, editors, and management to help determine what responsible AI stewardship looks like for their newsroom, whether they are looking to procure an AI tool or create their own. This may seem like a lot of work upfront for what otherwise might be a simple process. Answering these questions at the outset, however, will save newsrooms a lot of time and energy compared to retroactively figuring out responsible use of a tool after purchasing it, training it, and using it.

Note: Responsible procurement and use of AI tools requires understanding the ethical implications of such tools.

Scope limitations of this guide

Introducing AI technology in journalism requires internal management and preparation in the newsroom—not only for technical skills, but also for the cultural change it requires, taking into account the emotional needs and morale of those in the newsroom. The Guide **does not** touch upon the organizational and cultural impact of AI adoption, but we would like to note that it is an important consideration that is required to ensure the success of AI adoption in a newsroom. Journalists and team members should feel comfortable using the tool as an aid, not as a replacement for their work. In addition, it is important that journalists can provide their input into decision-making processes and have a real say in the AI tools chosen to aid in their work. For more on this, we encourage you to utilize PAI's Guidelines for AI & Shared Prosperity and refer to our report on AI and Job Quality.

What are AI tools for newsrooms?

Key terms

Broadly, AI tools are any technologies, software, or platforms that utilize algorithms or artificial intelligence to analyze data, automate processes, or make predictions or recommendations. While there are many definitions of AI, AI is, in essence, software systems that take in data, learn from that data, and interpret it.

Machine Learning

As defined by the General Services Administration, the practice of using algorithms that are able to learn from large datasets by extracting patterns, enabling the algorithm to take an iterative and adaptive approach to problem-solving.

Generative AI

A type of AI that can produce new content in various formats—including text, imagery, audio, or data—based on user inputs and the datasets it has been trained on.

Natural Language Generation

As described by IBM, the process of converting structured data into human-like text.

Natural Language Processing

As described by IBM, the ability of a machine to interpret what humans are saying through text or voice formats.

Computer Vision

A type of AI that seeks to classify or identify objects, features, or people in images or videos.

AI Bias

A prejudiced determination made by an AI system, particularly when it is inequitable or oppressive or impacts socially marginalized groups.

AI Ethics

The multidisciplinary field that aims to employ standards of moral conduct to consider the societal and ethical implications of algorithmic development and use.

Categories of AI tools for newsrooms

AI tools for newsrooms have various uses and can be used at different points in the news production process. To highlight this complexity, PAI analyzed more than 70 tools in our AI Tools for Local Newsrooms Database, providing plain-language descriptions of the AI tools and their uses and identifying five broad categories of AI tools relevant to journalists:

LEAD GENERATION TOOLS

Lead Generation Tools provide advance notice of trends, developing stories, or witness leads on breaking news. These tools can help journalists identify trending topics and potential sources on the scene.

CONTENT CREATION TOOLS

Content Creation Tools simplify and automate the news-writing and reporting process to help create content. Technologies like ChatGPT and other automated writing tools have made it increasingly easy to pull data and turn it into short articles about data-centric and factual content that requires editors' review before publishing.

AUDIENCE ENGAGEMENT TOOLS

Audience Engagement Tools focus on collecting data and moderating audience interactions and comments. These can be used to provide data on user behaviors and interests or tailor content to audiences. Audience engagement tools also include recommender systems, which can personalize news recommendations based on user preferences.

DISTRIBUTION TOOLS

Distribution Tools allow for a single piece of content to be shared in multiple languages or formats. Distribution tools can turn written content into audio, video, or images (and vice versa) or automate their distribution across many social media platforms.

INVESTIGATIVE AND DATA ANALYSIS TOOLS

Investigative and Data Analysis Tools support fact-finding and making sense of large datasets or a large number of documents. This makes it much easier to uncover patterns or hidden connections across documents, thereby reducing the amount of time and effort it takes to conduct investigative deep dives.

AI tools often have multiple features and can fall under multiple categories. For example, it is common for a tool to combine content creation and distribution functions. **Step 3** of this guide addresses the unique risks associated with utilizing each of these categories of tools.

Note: RESOURCE: AI Tools for Local Newsrooms Database.

How AI tools differ from other newsroom technologies

Several features differentiate AI tools from other software.

1. First, traditional software relies on a rules-based system where the outputs are the same every time. AI tools are iterative and often make decisions without explicit programming. Unlike with traditional software, we don't always have insight into how AI systems arrive at their conclusions or the factors involved. AI tools therefore require an additional layer of oversight that might not have been previously necessary with traditional software that is "plug and play" and produces the same results using the same processes every time.
2. Second, AI tools might not have the needed context to arrive at the correct conclusion (for example, when live-translating content) and thus need to be provided with that context through human oversight.
3. Third, AI tools may produce harmful outputs either unintentionally or through targeted attacks. While traditional software can suffer from similar vulnerabilities, the risk is amplified for AI tools. In turn, AI tools require that you continuously monitor how they operate, to ensure they continue to produce outputs that still align with their intended purposes.

These elements help justify the need for additional attention and governance when newsrooms adopt AI tools. This includes monitoring how data is being used to train models, the impact of those models, and determining thresholds for when tools are in need of retirement—all details described in more depth in the Guide.

Note: We don't always have insight into how AI systems arrive at their conclusions or the factors involved. AI tools therefore require an additional layer of oversight.

5 key principles for AI-adopting newsrooms

The step-by-step Guide below is informed by a set of recommendations for the ethical adoption of AI by newsrooms previously published by PAI. These principles are:

1. Newsrooms need clear goals for adopting AI tools
2. Technology must embody the standards and values of the news operation
3. Transparency, explainability, and accountability mechanisms must accompany the implementation of AI tools
4. Newsroom staff need to actively supervise AI tools
5. Distribution platforms must embed journalistic values into their AI systems

For a more in-depth understanding of these recommendations please read PAI's blog post on the topic.

Note: READ MORE: Local Newsrooms Should Adopt AI Ethics as They Adopt AI: Five Recommendations

10 steps for AI adoption in newsrooms

AI Adoption for Newsrooms recommends newsrooms follow a 10-step process for adopting AI tools.

Working through the steps, if you discover by Step 2 that your newsroom's needs won't be addressed by an AI tool but are instead structural or organizational, consider addressing those first before proceeding. If by Steps 6 and 7, you find none of the AI tools meet your needs, **hold off on adopting an AI tool.** The sunk cost of time spent researching and testing out a tool is likely far smaller than implementing one that doesn't meet your needs or doesn't meet the standards for responsible AI that you've set.

1	Identify tasks that can be aided by an AI tool and who the tools are for	**2**	Map out your news operation cycle and where an AI tool might fit into existing systems
3	Pinpoint the category of tools you'll be considering	**4**	Consult the AI tools database and establish performance benchmarks
5	Shortlist three to five potential AI tools and questions you'd ask the developers	**6**	Select one or two tools that you would like to procure
7	Clearly outline the potential benefits and drawbacks of implementing this tool	**8**	Set up your newsroom for success after procurement
9	Understand the lifecycle of an AI tool	**10**	Determine when you should retire an AI tool

1 *Identify the outcomes and objectives of adding an AI tool*

What opportunities exist in your newsroom for greater efficiencies, faster news production, or better audience engagement? What are the current gaps or improvements that your newsroom is hoping to address?

First, identify the key objectives or outcomes your newsroom is attempting to improve upon. Then, where additional technology and automation can support addressing those objectives, bolster the work already being done in the newsroom or provide avenues for new coverage in the newsroom.

Consult the journalists in your newsroom who will be using the tool as a first step to identifying gaps or pain points that can be supported by AI tools. In addition, bringing together members of the product, tech, and editorial teams (where applicable) in consultation is important to ensure that all views are represented when considering an AI tool. Doing so ensures that the technology is in fact needed by the newsroom, and that it will address an existing problem or aid in the newsroom's sustainability or growth.

Choose a technology based on clear indications that it: (a) will be an investment in the newsroom's sustainability or growth, and (b) is addressing clear objectives. This ensures that the time spent choosing the tool, adding it to the news production process, and any accompanying training required for its use is time well spent. Throughout the tool's lifecycle, return to the objectives identified in this step to determine if the tool continues to meet its original objectives, or if it is no longer needed and can be retired (see **Step 10**: Determine When You Should Retire an AI Tool).

Note: Consult the journalists in your newsroom who will be using the tool as a first step to identifying gaps or pain points that can be supported by AI tools.

QUESTIONS TO CONSIDER

The following questions can help identify the objectives and opportunities an AI tool addresses:

- **Is there an area of work where your newsroom does not have enough support?**

  In many newsrooms, this may be social media distribution or creating content in multiple formats to expand the reach of the newsroom from written content to podcasts or videos that can be shared on social media. There might not be a dedicated person responsible for content creation, but an AI tool might support that capability in a newsroom (and should include human oversight).

- **Are there repetitive tasks that take place in the news production or distribution process that can otherwise be automated?**

  Repetitive tasks may be a starting point for automation as they can alleviate the burden for journalists and give them time back to accomplish more complex work.

- **Is there a category of tools that your newsroom is particularly excited about? Why?**

  Sometimes it may be easier to look at what tools your newsroom would be excited to integrate (as long as they still fulfill a need in your newsroom). These tools may not address your newsroom's most pressing needs. However, it may enhance your newsroom's adoption and acceptance of AI tools more broadly, and help demonstrate their efficacy in other, perhaps related, contexts.

 Map out your news production cycle and where an AI tool might fit into existing systems

Start by mapping out what the typical news production pipeline looks like for your newsroom, from ideation to publishing and marketing. This process mapping exercise will support the adoption of an AI tool by allowing you to consider where the tool would be added in your news production cycle before procurement. To streamline the tool's implementation, determine where the tool will be added to the news production process and communicate that with team members positioned to use or make decisions related to the use of the tool. This is an important step that will set you up for success for the remainder of the adoption process.

In addition, mapping the news production cycle and where an AI tool will be added helps identify the primary use case for the AI tool. Consequently, narrowing down the primary use case for the tool will make it much easier to find the tool that makes sense for your newsroom. It's not necessarily the cheapest, best-marketed, or most feature-rich tool, but rather the one that makes the most sense for your team's needs at the moment.

For example, your newsroom might have identified a need for a translation tool to reach a wider audience in your community. Mapping out the news production cycle will help determine when the translation should occur and who will be verifying that translation is accurate.

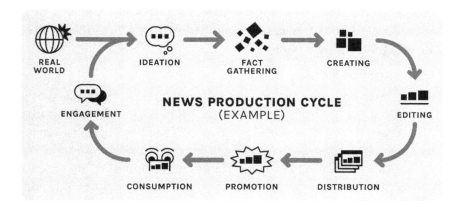

NEWS PRODUCTION CYCLE
(EXAMPLE)

REAL WORLD → IDEATION → FACT GATHERING → CREATING → EDITING → DISTRIBUTION → PROMOTION → CONSUMPTION → ENGAGEMENT

Note: Mapping the news production cycle and where an AI tool will be added helps identify the primary use case for the AI tool.

 Pinpoint the category of tools you'll be considering and understand the associated risks

Choose a category of tools to help you more easily identify potential benefits and risks of its use while also narrowing down your choices from the variety of AI tools available to newsrooms.

We have identified five broad categories of AI tools that may assist newsrooms. By starting with these broad categories, newsrooms can begin narrowing down the appropriate AI tools to consider.

Note: Choosing a category of tools helps you more easily identify potential benefits and risks.

3.1 Risks associated with various AI tool categories

In "Sketching the Field of AI Tools for Local Newsrooms," PAI identifies potential downsides associated with each of these categories, information we've summarized below that must be considered when evaluating these tools:

Note: READ MORE: Sketching the Field of AI Tools for Local Newsrooms; Local Newsrooms Should Adopt AI Ethics as They Adopt AI: Five Recommendations

LEAD GENERATION

Lead generation tools can help provide early notice of trends, developing stories, or sources for breaking news. However, these tools may only surface national or state-level trends. Trending topics can mask local news stories that are important to readers interested in learning more about their city or town. If local newsrooms are not careful, they could overlook providing local insights (their biggest value add) in favor of covering trending stories. Additionally, **any algorithmic tool that draws on large datasets (like social media posts) poses questions about consent that may go beyond the established ethical codes of journalism.**

CONTENT CREATION

Content creation tools are used to simplify and automate the news-writing process. When working with such tools, however, **errors in data auto-populated into a database can result in much larger errors in the news articles published.** Automated reporting can also lack very important context or information, giving the audience an incomplete picture of the story. Consequently, newsrooms may be providing audiences with incomplete or disjointed pieces of information, inadvertently spreading misinformation or letting readers fill in the gaps in reporting with their own biases.

AUDIENCE ENGAGEMENT

Audience engagement tools are focused on managing interactions, newsletters, and comments. However, **personalized news delivery relies very heavily on collecting data from individual users.** It can be unclear who has access to the data, how it is stored, or if it is being sold to other marketing platforms. There is often limited clarity on whether the audience has provided informed consent for their data to be collected and shared for that purpose. Over-reliance on limited audience data can also provide an incomplete picture of audience behaviors or preferences. This can be detrimental to the public interest goals of a newsroom in the long run, either exposing their audience to a very limited number of news categories or creating news echo chambers.

Note: READ MORE: Fairer Algorithmic Decision-Making and Its Consequences; Knowing the Risks: A Necessary Step to Using Demographic Data for Algorithmic Fairness.

DISTRIBUTION

Distribution tools ensure that a single piece of content can be shared in many languages or in a variety of formats. **Auto-translation (though fast and potentially helpful) needs to be reviewed for context-specific translation, accuracy, and cultural sensitivity.** Therefore, it's important to keep a human in the loop, specifically a native speaker and/or experienced translator, to review those translations prior to publication. In addition, transforming news content into new formats can bring its own host of ethical considerations, such as questions of copyright and where the voice or video is being sourced.

Note: READ MORE: A Field Guide to Making AI Art Responsibly

INVESTIGATIVE AND DATA ANALYSIS

Investigative tools support fact-finding and data analysis, especially when trying to make sense of large datasets or a large number of documents. **Investigative tools, while very sophisticated, are still prone to error if the data sources are not carefully interrogated.** The data sources, parameters provided to the algorithm, or assumptions made by the reporter need to be interrogated to ensure that the data analysis is not biased and that the conclusions are sound. In addition, it is important that these stories are provided with appropriate context as to how the data was obtained and the methodology through which the findings were reached.

Note: WATCH MORE: Bridging AI Ethics and Journalistic Standards

3.2 Adopt one tool at a time

We highly recommend that newsrooms deploy one tool at a time and start with phased rollouts (that is, not with whole systems-level change), especially if this is the first AI tool your newsroom is adopting. Look at areas where automation can support pre-existing and repetitive work. It may be tempting to adopt more than one tool at once to provide additional support to your newsroom or address long-standing issues. Instead, we recommend you adopt one AI tool at a time. Once you've picked that tool, start by piloting its adoption with one team first and then phasing the roll-out across your newsroom. That way, the disruption to your news production is minimized and any issues with the use of the tool can be addressed early on. Furthermore, it gives your newsroom the opportunity to adjust to the changes and the idea of including AI tools in news production. It also mitigates unanticipated impacts that would otherwise be widespread.

Note: We highly recommend that newsrooms deploy one tool at a time.

3.3 Recommended starting point

Distribution tools can expand the reach of the newsroom and its audience, providing a quick value add for a newsroom. Distribution tools perform tasks that may be particularly helpful because social media manager, content creator, and translator roles are often understaffed or even non-existent in local newsrooms.

Being able to translate a newsroom's content into multiple languages to meet the local population's needs can exponentially expand reach. Being able to offer content in multiple formats such as transforming written articles into audio podcasts or short videos can expand a newsroom's social media presence and reach as well.

USE CASE

The *Brainerd Dispatch* and Michigan Radio use AI tools to cut down monitoring and transcription time

In March 2023, Renee Richardson of the *Brainerd Dispatch* told The Monitor about her newsroom's motivation for adopting AI.

"We're constantly asking our staff to do more and provide more information in many more ways," said Richardson. "Whether that be social media, video podcasts, audio segments, all of our photography, or all those pieces that go into it. Rarely do we do much that gives them time back. The benefit I see for this is finally giving them that time back."

Richardson told The Monitor that the *Brainerd Dispatch* is building an AI program to automate police public safety announcements, a system intended to give journalists time back to work on reporting.

The hope is that the *Brainerd Dispatch* can cut down on time required to monitor police blotters in the same way that reporters at Michigan Radio WUOM-FM have been able to use an AI transcription tool to create transcripts of City Council and Subcommittee meetings in over 40 cities. "It allows a reporter like me to get a lot more coverage to the audience than I could just doing it by myself," Dustin Dwyer told The Monitor. The transcriptions aren't perfect and need to be reviewed by the reporters for accuracy, but they provide a starting point for reporting on important City Council issues without having to sit through hours of meetings.

Note: READ MORE: Can AI programs be trusted to report the news?

 Establish performance benchmarks

If you've made it to Step 4, you've identified the objectives you'd like an AI tool to support, where it would fit into your news production cycle, and the broad category of tools under consideration. The next step is to benchmark your newsroom's current performance in the area the tool will be used so you can compare a few tool options.

Establishing a baseline or benchmark for your current newsroom's performance will help you determine if those tools can support your newsroom's improvement in that area.

Benchmarks also help you measure the efficacy of the tool once you've implemented it because they set a baseline for your newsroom's performance in a particular area prior to AI adoption. The benchmarks selected should also flow from the objectives identified for the use of an AI tool in **Step 1**. What are the measurable ways you can assess whether the identified objectives are being fulfilled? How do these compare to industry standards or those of other newsrooms?

Note: Establishing a baseline or benchmark will help you determine if those tools can support your newsroom's improvement.

Note: READ MORE: Six steps to create a metrics-driven newsroom

QUESTIONS TO CONSIDER

The following questions can be a great starting point and can lead you to metrics that can be developed into benchmarks moving forward:

- How does your audience come across your content at the moment?

- How does your audience interact with your content? For instance: click on links within it, reads through to the end, or shares the content with others

- What type of content is your audience most or least interested in?

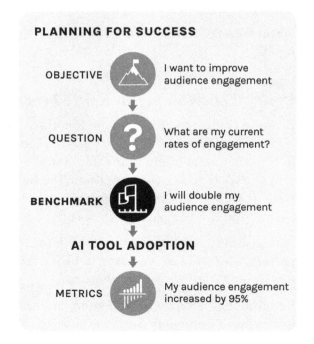

PLANNING FOR SUCCESS

OBJECTIVE — I want to improve audience engagement

QUESTION — What are my current rates of engagement?

BENCHMARK — I will double my audience engagement

AI TOOL ADOPTION

METRICS — My audience engagement increased by 95%

- What is the demographic diversity of your audience?

- How much time does it take to produce your current content?

- How many content items are produced for your audience daily, weekly or monthly?

 ## *Shortlist three to five potential AI tools and interview the tool developers*

After establishing benchmarks for your newsroom, consult PAI's AI Tools for Local Newsrooms Database as well as conduct your own research as to which tools might be best-suited to meet the needs identified in **Steps 1–3**.

From the AI tools available, choose three to five potential tools you'd like to explore.

The database provides a great starting point, particularly given the many sorting filters available. However, you would also benefit from consulting with other newsrooms to find out which tools they're using and conducting your own research. JournalismAI has surveyed and collected use cases of newsrooms that have used AI to support their work.

Shortlisting three to five tools will help make it easier to really vet each tool, interview its developers, and make an informed decision about which is best-suited for the needs of your newsroom. After you've created that list, **reach out to each of the vendors for a demo** before you make any decisions. Most of their websites will provide a way to request a demo and further discuss how the tool can work for you.

Make sure to take note of the various uses of any tool considered, since it likely can achieve various outcomes. Compare the uses provided to the objective or outcome you've identified in **Step 1**.

What are the gaps between the needs you've identified for your newsroom and the services that the tool provides? Some tools require further customization to fit your newsroom's needs. It is imperative that you spend time asking all the questions and understanding all the ways in which the tool can work for you, the associated costs, and any ethical considerations you should keep in mind during implementation. Ethical considerations about AI implementation—such as fairness, transparency and accountability—should be thought of as an extension of journalistic ethics. As such, understanding a tool completely by asking the right questions will allow you to make the appropriate evaluation of whether it embodies the standards and values of the news operation.

Procurements can take three calls or more with the developer to truly understand the tool and ask all of your questions, so make sure that you factor that time into the process.

Below, we've included a list of questions to ask in a demo. Depending on the type of tool you're considering, its level of sophistication, and how embedded it will be in your newsroom, omit or add to them as necessary.

Note: Spend time asking all the questions and understanding all the ways in which the tool can work for you, the associated costs, and any ethical considerations.

Note: RESOURCES: AI Tools for Local Newsrooms Database; Journalism AI Case Studies; Generating Change: A global survey of what news organizations are doing with artificial intelligence

QUESTIONS TO CONSIDER

Questions you can ask in an AI tool demo:

- **What is the core offering of this tool? What was the primary use case it was designed for?**
  Most tools will have a core offering that it was originally intended for along with add-on features that were added later. It is important that you understand the original purpose of the AI tool because that is what the tool will be optimized for.

172

- **Are there additional customizations that will be needed for the tool to be used or are you able to put it to work right away?**

  What control does your newsroom have over customizations?

  What control levers can your newsrooms continue to adjust in the use of the tool after its launch?

- **If additional customization/programming is needed, is the expertise to do so available on your team? Are the AI tool developers able to aid with the process?**

- **Are tool customizations saved locally or deployed globally in the tool?**

  Are any customizations made by you to the AI tool then deployed across the various users of the tool in your organization or are they kept specific to each use?

  Can any customizations made by your organizations be reused by the tool developers?

- **What is the cost of procurement? Is it a recurring or one-time cost?**

- **Does the tool require frequent updates?**

  This question will help you determine how often you might need to stop and update the tool and how that might affect your workflow.

- **How do you monitor its efficacy? Are there metrics that are provided by the tool to track its outcomes?**

- **Has the tool been used by other newsrooms? Can the developers provide use cases or examples?**

  This question will provide practical insight into the reality of using this tool. If neither can be provided by the developers, then perhaps it might be worth questioning the efficacy and claims made by the tool developers.

  Are you able to get in touch with these newsrooms to ask about their experience?

- **What liability might the newsroom incur when using this AI tool?**
  This is an important question to help identify any privacy or copyright implications of using this tool and glean if the tool developers have actively worked to address and/or support users with such concerns.

- **What data does the AI-developing company collect through the tool when it's deployed? Is any of the data collected personal information? How might that data be reused?**
  Questions on data collection, storage, and reuse will help you determine if this tool meets the ethical values set by your newsroom.

- **Is there any consent that should be obtained from the audience if and when they're interacting with the tool? Is this collected and embedded in the tool, or should you develop your own consent protocol?**

- **How is the company funded and how does the company make money? What other industries does it serve?**

- **What notification will the AI company provide in the event that there are shifts to the business model?**
  The company may choose to switch its business model or focus down the line from being a newsroom-dedicated product to targeting a different industry. It is important to know if they will notify you of such change and if that industry is acceptable to your newsroom standards. For example, sometimes the AI tool can be used for surveillance purposes or policing as an alternative use case.

- **Are there any ethical considerations that were explored by the developer when creating this tool? What mitigations, if any, have they put in place as a result?**

Note: Understand the original purpose of the AI tool because that is what the tool will be optimized for.

Note: Questions on data collection, storage, and reuse will help you determine if a tool meets the ethical values set by your newsroom.

Note: RESOURCE: Annotation and Benchmarking on Understanding and Transparency of Machine Learning Lifecycles (ABOUT ML)

6 *Select one to two tools you'd like to procure*

Use the responses to the questions posed in **Step 5** to **eliminate tools that do not meet your requirements** and that should narrow your focus to one to two tools.

There will likely be additional considerations that are unique to your newsroom that will factor into your decision-making, such as the cost of the tool, the capacity for and anticipated speed of implementation, or if your newsroom has the expertise for oversight. From there, land on one to two tools that you'd like to shortlist for adoption, from the three to five in earlier stages of the Guide.

If no tools meet your requirements, it might be best to hold off on proceeding further instead of just "making a tool work" for the time being. Technological path dependency* makes it increasingly difficult to swap tools after you've invested time and money in adoption, training, and incorporating one effectively, making your newsroom operation dependent on it. This is a hazard for newsrooms and therefore it is better to hold off implementing a tool until you find one that is best for your organization in the long run.

Note: If no tools meet your requirements, it might be best to hold off on proceeding further.

Note: *"Technological path dependency" is when organizations continue using a tool because they've invested money and time in adoption, training, and incorporating it—even when it is not the best option.

7 *Outline the potential benefits and drawbacks of implementing this tool*

Now that you've chosen your top tool, it's time to turn to implementation considerations within your newsroom. To plan for implementation, **it is important to be clear about how the tool will be used** within the newsroom and the oversight that will be required. Even the most responsible and ethical tool cannot be implemented without continuous oversight of its use and outputs. In order to appropriately gauge all the above, and put in the mechanisms to mitigate any negative outcomes, you must first understand what those outcomes might be.

A thorough vetting process ensures that leadership and staff are aligned when it comes to opportunities, objectives, and risks. Furthermore, it provides clarity on **how any risks can be mitigated by your newsroom.**

Note: Ultimately, the newsroom should consider the trade-offs between the business opportunities and the ethical considerations.

Note: READ MORE: Sketching the Field of AI Tools for Local Newsrooms

QUESTIONS TO CONSIDER

Questions to consider when creating the list of opportunities and risks to mitigate:

- **How should we be transparent about the use of this tool?** Transparency with newsroom staff members and audience is key when using AI tools that are collecting their data (similar to web cookies) or that are supporting the production or prioritization of content that they are seeing. This maintains the newsroom's credibility and ensures that the audience isn't caught off guard should they find out that the content they're consuming isn't human-generated. Consider experimenting with new ways for describing the use of these tools transparently, especially as disclosure methods are continually iterated upon.

Some would argue that backend AI tools—such as data analysis tools, transcription tools, or summarization tools—don't need to be disclosed to the audience as they do not directly impact them. However, newsrooms have often benefited from disclosing the AI tools they use that are not explicitly user-facing simply for the purpose of being transparent with their audiences and to be able to exchange insights with other newsrooms. For example, the *New York Times* shared with its audience how they're using machine learning to determine their paywall strategy.

- **How might this tool or product negatively impact our audience's privacy?**
  Is this tool collecting personal information about your readers? Is any of that data unnecessary? How can the data be misused to potentially negatively impact your audience?

  Can the data be de-anonymized? Depending on the geographical area you're in and the population density, can the granularity of the data make individuals identifiable?

- **How might this tool or product require us to acquire or retain personal information or make inferences about our readers that could produce harms, such as discrimination?**
  Can the data being collected reveal identifying information about each user? Will this data be reused for marketing or other purposes in the newsroom?

- **How might this tool or product reduce audiences' autonomy in seeking information or perspectives?**
  Is this tool inadvertently narrowing the diversity of news available to our audience? If so, how might we ensure that news selection exposes them to a diverse selection of news and provides the audience with an opportunity to choose differently?

- **How might this tool or product change our cost structure in ways that force us to pass costs to the reader, potentially impacting engagement and/or the bottom line?**
  Will the cost of the tool inevitably cause us to increase subscription prices or create a paywall that limits readership?

- **Do promises in the marketing language for this tool or product go beyond what is realistically achievable by the state of the art?**
  It's important to be realistic about the expectations that newsroom leadership and staff have about the tool and what it can deliver. This will help you accurately set metrics and expectations in the newsroom.

- **How do we account for potential inaccuracies and representation biases produced by automated systems and maintain our editorial integrity?**
  This question helps identify any potential checks and balances that need to be placed in the newsroom to ensure that there is journalistic oversight over what is produced using AI tools. This ensures that at no point does technological dependency overtake journalistic integrity, either intentionally or unintentionally.

- **Does this tool change our relationship with our staff in ways that might negatively impact our culture, hiring, or staff relations?**
  This question points to broader considerations about the impact of introducing an AI tool on the newsroom's culture. Will members of the newsroom feel threatened by the use of the tool? How will their fears be assuaged? Will its use be mandatory?

- **Are there implementation challenges that might be unique to your newsroom?**
  Every newsroom is different and starting from a different place for technical preparedness and infrastructure. Consider how that might affect implementation—for example, if the

computers in your newsroom are not powerful enough to handle the AI tools you procure that would render them ineffective.

- **What other entities does the vendor contract with? What conflicts might that create?**
  Similar to the question in **Step 6**, knowing what other industries the provider caters to can help you make decisions about how the data and information collected by the provider might be reused and if that is aligned with your newsroom's ethical standards.

- **How does acquiring this tool or product make us more or less reliant on tech firms and external providers that may not share our values?**
  How does relying on AI tools' output, and specifically generative AI, impact the quality of the journalism produced?

- **What is a best-case and worst-case scenario of using the tool?**
  What might the worst-case scenario look like and do you have an exit ramp for the tool?

Note: READ MORE: Why watermarking AI-generated content won't guarantee trust online; How *The New York Times* Uses Machine Learning To Make Its Paywall Smarter; Demographic-Reliant Algorithmic Fairness: Characterizing the Risks of Demographic Data Collection in the Pursuit of Fairness

Taken collectively, the answers to the questions above should provide the newsroom with a final checkpoint to make a decision about whether to proceed with procurement. The assessment provided in this step and through the questions asked in **Step 6** should give a newsroom a clear idea of the benefits, risks, and requirements for oversight and mitigation. The newsroom can then decide if:

- Costs are appropriate for the promised benefits
- The tool can be implemented ethically and responsibly
- Mitigation of risks and oversight are a responsibility the newsroom can appropriately take on

Ultimately, the newsroom should consider the tradeoffs between the business opportunities that using the AI tool provides and the ethical considerations of how the use of the tool will impact the newsroom staff, audiences, and news production.

Note: The assessment should give a newsroom a clear idea of the benefits, risks, and requirements for oversight and mitigation.

USE CASE

Lost Coast Outpost limited the use of its AI tool to mitigate risks

According to *The Monitor*, Lost Coast Outpost—a local newsroom in Humboldt County, California—built LoCOBot, an AI tool capable of scraping, summarizing, and writing articles (using ChatGPT) from City Council meeting minutes. Lost Coast elected to use the bot exclusively to scrape and summarize the meeting minutes. Lost Coast told the Monitor that it has chosen to continue being cautious and transparent with its audiences as well, labeling any work that is performed by the program.

Note: READ MORE: Can AI programs be trusted to report the news?

USE CASE

CNET's implementation of an AI tool without appropriate oversight led to widespread misreporting

News outlets, including Futurism, reported extensively on CNET's use of AI to produce written articles and its failure to disclose this approach to its audiences. When the news first broke in January of 2023, many journalists documented their dismay at the lack of disclosure and the misuse of AI in the journalistic context. In particular, CNET was using automated writers for detailed explainers and long-form writing as opposed to regular reporting on more data-driven insights, like sports results or real estate prices as some other outlets do. Articles written using factual data points such as sports scores tend to be short, providing only information on the game results and standings. This makes them less prone to mistakes as the AI writer is simply reformatting the data provided into fact-based sentences on game results.

CNET responded by adding bylines referencing AI as the author to previous articles where AI had been involved in writing the content as well as disclaimers at the onset of the article to that effect. Later, The Verge reported that CNET also used AI-generated content to re-write some of its published articles to increase their visibility on search engines, since optimizing language for algorithmic distribution can support engagement. Oftentimes, this left the article with disjointed pieces of content. According to The Verge, an editor from CNET would review the content to make sure the article makes sense and to remove any misinformation, but often did so months after publishing, limiting the effectiveness of the review. The Verge conducted a thorough investigation on CNET outlining the many ways AI tools were mismanaged by the news outlet, leading to misreporting and overall mistrust by its journalists and audiences.

If CNET had better governance in place for how the tool ought to be used and disclosed to the audiences when an article was written or updated by an automated writer, they would have operated more responsibly and likely received less backlash. Transparency with their audiences would have also allowed them to receive meaningful, productive feedback from readers and experts in the field alike on how they are using AI in the newsroom and where using automated writing is acceptable.

Note: READ MORE: CNET Secretly Used AI on Articles That Didn't Disclose That Face, Staff Say; Internet Horrified by CNET Secretively Publishing Articles Written by an AI; Inside CNET's AI-powered SEO money machine

8 *Set up your newsroom for success after procurement*

Now that you've decided on the tool, procured it, and outlined benefits and drawbacks to its use, there are a few more governance and measurement mechanisms to put in place in your organization. This step focuses on the **questions to ask to establish appropriate governance and develop sound metrics** to determine the AI tool's impact.

Note: Governance helps set a newsroom up for success, helping newsrooms measure the efficacy of the tool and its impact.

Decide:

1. **Who is primarily responsible for the tool and its use**

   It is imperative that a single person be identified in the newsroom as responsible for decision-making and oversight of the use of an AI tool. This ensures that there are clear lines of accountability within the newsroom and, should the AI tool make mistakes, it is clear who to contact to make changes.

2. **Who will be able to use the tool in your newsroom**

3. **What metrics you will track to determine the efficacy of the tool**

4. **What happens when things go wrong, what is the course correction, and what is the communication plan**

5. **If you can pilot the AI tool before implementing it across the board**

   This ensures that any governance questions that have not been addressed are considered in the pilot and any previously unaccounted for risks are mitigated. Furthermore, this ensures that staff get a chance to familiarize themselves with the tool before it's implemented across all news stories.

6. **How you will measure the efficacy of the transparency measures adopted in Step 7**

   The transparency measures adopted in **Step 7** should be monitored for their efficacy to understand how your audience is responding to them. It is important to measure if they are effective in conveying to your audience when AI is being used, especially as it impacts the content they're seeing.

Putting in place avenues for feedback from both the newsroom staff and from the public will help glean how they're receiving those transparency measures.

7. **What the necessary changes are in your newsroom (such as workflow redesign and retraining) to ensure the successful launch of the tool**

8. **What mechanisms you will have to collect feedback on the use of the tool from the users in your newsroom or from audiences**

9. **What methods of redress you will provide for your audience and staff members to provide feedback/report errors on the use (or misuse) of the tool**

Governance helps set a newsroom up for success, helping newsrooms measure the efficacy of the tool and its impact. The next section outlines various ways a newsroom can measure the efficacy and impact of a tool on a continual basis.

8.1 Metrics and efficacy

Measuring the tool's efficacy serves dual purposes: it helps ensure that the tool is operating ethically and responsibly using quantifiable metrics and it also allows you to track the business outcomes your newsroom hoped to achieve from adopting this tool.

To get started on measuring the efficacy of the tool, you should consider two pieces of information that you should have been previously collecting (see **Steps 4 and 5**):

1. The baseline benchmarks of how your newsroom previously performed prior to using the tool
2. The metrics and data points that the tool provider has built in or tracks as part of the tool

Once considered, decide what additional metrics you'd like to collect to provide insight into the tool's performance and how it's impacting your overall newsroom goals. These metrics will flow from the initial outcome you've identified for the use of this AI tool in **Step 1**.

This section focuses on new metrics that can be collected due to the use of a particular AI tool which provides new opportunities for oversight and measurement, in contrast to benchmarks which help you measure the baseline of where your newsroom has started and how that compares to the improvements made as you use a new AI tool.

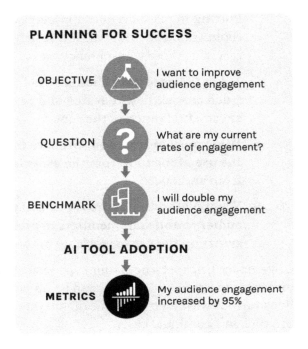

METRICS TO CONSIDER

Start by asking what the best way to measure the outcome is and what evidence there may be in your newsroom (both qualitative and quantitative) to prove this. Below are some of the areas of measurement used by other newsrooms:

- Accuracy measures how well the AI tool is able to perform its intended function without errors. For example, an AI tool designed to write articles using data inputs should be able to do so without misinforming the audience or adding inaccurate context to the written article.

- Precision measures how precise the AI tool is in its results. For example, how often does it correctly identify a piece of information as fake? The rate of both false positives and negatives should be considered when assessing precision.

- Recall measures the portion of relevant results that the AI tool is able to return. For example, if you're querying an AI tool for a particular piece of information out of a large data set, is it able to accurately recall all the relevant information related to the query in the database?

- Efficiency measures the time savings from using an AI tool.

- User satisfaction measures how satisfied the users of the AI tool are with its performance. This can be collected directly from journalists who are using the tool in their day-to-day work, perhaps through qualitative surveys.

- **Cost-effectiveness** measures how cost-effective the AI tool is compared to other solutions. Here, cost encompasses both the direct cost of the tool and the indirect cost of training staff and integrating the tool into existing workflows.

- **Audience engagement** measures how well a tool directed at the audience is increasing engagement with the news. This can include online comments, emails, and newsletter signups.

- **Conversion** measures how the AI tool is increasing subscriptions and overall revenue for the newsroom.

NOTE: READ MORE: Classification: True vs. False and Positive vs. Negative; Evaluating the efficacy of AI content detection tools in differentiating between human and AI-generated text

In addition to the above categories, there might be cascading effects worth tracking to get a better idea of a tool's impact. For example, if you are using a translation tool in order to reach a wider audience, the tool itself might not track your new readership as a result of using the tool. However, your newsroom likely internally tracks the readership and their broad geographical location. Comparing the baseline readership metrics prior to translating the content and after might give you an idea of the additional audience engagement provided by the tool. Going a step further might include adding a survey for the translated article asking for feedback on the accuracy of the translation and how it can be improved. That way, you're getting a deeper understanding not just of the impact of the AI tool on your audience, but also its accuracy in delivering the correct interpretation and news to your audience.

Lastly, we'd recommend that you **limit the number of vanity metrics*** used to measure efficacy. Metrics such as open rates for newsletters or traffic on a website look great on paper, but alone they might not provide a complete picture of how an AI tool is actually supporting a newsroom or meeting the expectations set out in **Step 1**.

Note: *Vanity metrics are metrics that are easily obtainable, easily understandable, and can seem to showcase success over time—such as likes and shares on a social media post. However, they do not provide an accurate portrayal of the return on investment from using a particular tool, as they only reflect surface-level audience engagement.

9 *Understand the lifecycle of an AI tool*

AI tools regularly incorporate new data inputs, can be customized to the needs of each newsroom, and develop over time. This means that their outputs and behavior can also change. As your newsroom continues to use a tool, it's important to audit the inputs, data collection, and output of the tool to ensure that it continues to yield the intended results. Mitigating risk early on helps support the continued use of a tool and can help ensure that negative or unwanted outputs don't appear later on. However, **that doesn't take away the need to continually monitor the tool**, any updates that have been issued by the developer, and any changes to the ways in which the data is being collected or used.

This is where the role of the person designated with oversight in **Step 8** becomes particularly crucial. They will be responsible for monitoring not just the outputs of the tool, but also any changes or updates issued by the provider. This includes developer update emails that can unfortunately be quite lengthy and include a lot of fine print.

Buried within them might be important information about how the collection or use of data has changed, therefore implicating your newsroom.

In addition, continual maintenance of the tool—keeping it up-to-date and ensuring its outcomes continue to match its intended purpose— avoids future technical debt.*

Note: As your newsroom continues to use a tool, ensure that it continues to yield the intended results.

Note: *"Technical debt" occurs when teams delay updating features, fail to maintain functionality, or settle for suboptimal performance over time. These outcomes can be the result of a "if it's not broken, don't fix it" mentality.

QUESTIONS TO CONSIDER

Questions you might want to ask in your newsroom at this stage include:

- What does continual maintenance look like?

- Who will be responsible for future and continued communication with the tool provider?

- How can you ensure that the AI tool continues to operate as intended? At what frequency will you conduct audits of performance?

- If the tool has a regular subscription payment, tying the audit to the renewal of the subscription can build in a natural trigger for regular audits and ensure regular oversight before renewing the subscription.

- How will you be accounting for unintended consequences outlined in **Step 7**?

- Are there any other processes that need to be implemented to account for negative impacts of the tool or mitigate their impact?

10 *Determine when you should retire an AI tool*

Part of stewarding AI tools in your newsroom is knowing **when they are no longer serving their original purpose** or supporting your newsroom as defined in earlier steps.

The questions about the tool, its use, metrics, governance, and ethical guidelines in previous sections can be called upon perpetually when reviewing the tool. If the intended goals are no longer being met, or new ethical concerns arise, then there should be an established off-ramp process for retiring a tool from your newsroom.

It might not even be the functionality of the tool that has changed, but rather the intended use by its provider that has shifted or, perhaps, data being collected and reused has changed. In addition, the priorities or needs of your newsroom may have changed and therefore the tool is no longer serving those needs.

QUESTIONS TO CONSIDER

Some questions you might want to ask in your assessment:

- Has the primary use of this tool changed by the developer? Is that use in line with journalistic ethics?

- Is the governance and oversight of the AI tool by our newsroom sufficient to mitigate its potential adverse impacts? If not, are we able to adjust our oversight to meet these challenges?

- Does the cost-benefit analysis of using this tool still make sense for our newsroom? Are there other considerations we should now take into account?

All of these elements should be a cause for pause in newsrooms deciding whether to continue using a tool internally. Making the proactive decision to stop using a tool and being transparent with the audience about that decision allows your newsroom to better maintain its credibility with stakeholders, including the audience and staff. It also allows your newsroom to be intentional in its decisions about how it uses AI tools and mitigates associated risks, and to discontinue their use when they no longer serve their purpose. Following these steps with intention can help newsrooms navigate the implementation of AI, responsibly.

Note: There should be an established off-ramp process for retiring a tool from your newsroom.

Acknowledgments

AI Adoption for Newsrooms was iteratively developed by PAI's AI and Media Integrity team under comprehensive guidance from the AI and Local News Steering Committee. We'd like to thank the Steering Committee members for their commitment to this programmatic work and for their generosity in time, expertise, and effort to advance this project. Their astute contributions and detailed comments on earlier drafts have strengthened this work immensely.

We would also like to thank the Partnership on AI staff who championed this work and provided thoughtful feedback and ideas throughout the research and writing process: Claire Leibowicz, Stephanie Bell, Hudson Hongo and Neil Uhl.

Finally, PAI is grateful to the Knight Foundation for their financial support and thought partnership of the AI and local news work—and personally grateful to Marc Lavalee, Director of Technology, for his wisdom and energy.

If you would like to add to this work or to the list of resources available, to utilize this guide as part of your newsroom's journey, or just to be involved in our future work at the intersection of AI and news, please reach out to dalia@partnershiponai.org.

Chapter Notes

Chapter 1

1. "Alan Turing and the Beginning of AI." Britannica. https://www.britannica.com/technology/artificial-intelligence/Alan-Turing-and-the-beginning-of-AI.

2. "Alan Turing and the Beginning of AI."

3. Rockwell Anyoha. "The History of Artificial Intelligence." Harvard Science in the News, August 28, 2017. https://sitn.hms.harvard.edu/flash/2017/history-artificial-intelligence.

4. Investopedia Team. "Artificial Intelligence: What It Is and How It is Used." Updated April 9, 2024. https://www.investopedia.com/terms/a/artificial-intelligence-ai.asp.

5. Derick David. "AI Is the New Internet." Medium, April 21, 2020. https://medium.com/utopian/ai-is-the-new-internet-5ea3316e14dc.

6. "Artificial Intelligence: What It Is and How It is Used."

7. "Artificial Intelligence: What It Is and How It is Used."

8. George Lawton. "What is generative AI? Everything you need to know." TechTarget. https://www.techtarget.com/searchenterpriseai/definition/generative-AI.

9. Associated Press. "ChatGPT's Chief Testifies Before U.S. Congress as Concerns Grow about AI Risks." May 16, 2023. https://www.voanews.com/a/chatgpt-chief-testifies-before-us-congress-as-concerns-grow-about-ai-risks/7095657.html.

10. Gerrit De Vynck. "AI leaders warn congress that AI could be used to create bioweapons." *Washington Post*, July 25, 2023. https://www.washingtonpost.com/technology/2023/07/25/ai-bengio-anthropic-senate-hearing/.

11. Lori Ioannou. "Jim Goodnight, the 'Godfather of AI,' predicts the future fate of the U.S. workforce." CNBC, January 21, 2020. https://www.cnbc.com/2019/11/04/godfather-of-ai-predicts-the-future-fate-of-the-us-workforce.html.

12. Ian Bremer and Mustafa Suleyman. "The AI Power Paradox: Can States Learn to Govern Artificial Intelligence Before It's Too Late?" *Foreign Affairs*, September/October 2023. https://www.foreignaffairs.com/world/artificial-intelligence-power-paradox.

13. For perspective, see David Dunlap. "1896: Without Fear or Favor." *New York Times*, August 14, 2015. https://www.nytimes.com/2015/09/12/insider/1896-without-fear-or-favor.html.

Chapter 2

1. Associated Press. "Artificial Intelligence at the Associated Press." May 2023. https://www.ap.org/discover/artificial-intelligence. All subsequent references to AP's strategy and approach to AI are from this source.

2. S. Saad and T. Issa. "Integration or Replacement: Journalism in the Era of Artificial Intelligence and Robot Journalism." *International Journal of Media, Journalism and Mass Communications* (IJMJMC), Volume 6, Issue 3, 2020, pp. 01–13 ISSN 2454–9479. https://www.arcjournals.org/pdfs/ijmjmc/v6-i3/1.pdf.

3. J. Peiser. "The Rise of the Robot Reporter." *New York Times*, February 5,

2019. https://www.nytimes.com/2019/02/05/business/media/artificial-intelligence-journalism-robots.html.

4. Jessica Patterson. "Are we entering the age of artificial journalism intelligence?" Digital Context Next, March 9, 2023. https://digitalcontentnext.org/blog/2023/03/09/are-we-entering-the-age-of-artificial-journalistic-intelligence/.

5. Jon Christian. "C-Net's Article-Writing AI Is Already Publishing Very Dumb Errors." Futurism, January 29, 2023. https://futurism.com/cnet-ai-errors.

6. P. Farhi. "A website used AI to write news stories: it was a journalistic disaster." *Washington Post*, January 17, 2023. https://www.washingtonpost.com/media/2023/01/17/cnet-ai-articles-journalism-corrections/.

7. Connie Gugliemo. "CNET Is Testing an AI Engine. Here's What We've Learned, Mistakes and All." CNET, January 25, 2023. https://www.cnet.com/tech/cnet-is-testing-an-ai-engine-heres-what-weve-learned-mistakes-and-all/.

8. Julianna Lozada. "The Robot Reporter's Lukewarm Welcome into the Newsroom: Journalism Layoffs and Failed Experiments with AI." *Columbia Political Review*, July 21, 2023. http://www.cpreview.org/articles/2023/7/the-robot-reporters-lukewarm-welcome-into-the-newsroom-journalism-layoffs-and-failed-experiments-with-ai.

9. Quoted in Lozada.

10. Allison Carter. "Another journalism outlet flounders with challenges of AI." PR Daily, August 29, 2023. https://www.prdaily.com/gannett-ai-program-ends/.

11. Edward R. Murrow. "Wires and Lights in a Box." Speech at RTNDA convention, October 15, 1958. The full text of his speech can be found at https://www.rtdna.org/murrows-famous-wires-and-lights-in-a-box.

12. Lozada.

13. Bernard Marr. "The Intersection of AI and Human Creativity: Can Machines Really Be Creative?" *Forbes*, March 27, 2023. https://www.forbes.com/sites/bernardmarr/2023/03/27/the-intersection-of-ai-and-human-creativity-can-machines-really-be-creative.

14. Tojin Eapean, et al. "How Generative AI Can Augment Human Creativity." *Harvard Business Review*, July/August 2023. https://hbr.org/2023/07/how-generative-ai-can-augment-human-creativity.

15. Sheena Iyengar. "AI Could Help Free Human Creativity." *Time*, June 23, 2023. https://time.com/6289278/ai-affect-human-creativity/.

Chapter 3

1. Michelle Cyca. "Nostalgia about Newsrooms Ignores How Much They Need to Change." The Walrus, January 8, 2024. https://thewalrus.ca/nostalgia-about-newsrooms-ignores-how-much-they-need-to-change/.

2. John Crowley. "What will newsrooms look like after the pandemic is over?" Journalism.co.uk, April 17, 2020. https://www.journalism.co.uk/news-commentary/what-will-the-newsrooms-look-like-after-the-pandemic-is-over-/s6/a754615.

3. Somini Sengupta. "AI is spying on the food we throw away." *New York Times*, April 4, 2024. Retrieved from https://www.nytimes.com/2024/04/04/climate/artificial-intelligence-food-waste.html.

4. Samuel Danzon-Chambaud. "Covering Covid-19 with automated news." *Columbia Journalism Review*, April 6, 2021. Retrieved from https://www.cjr.org/tow_center_reports/covering-covid-automated-news.php.

5. Rocky Parker. "AI in the newsroom: These outlets aren't spooked." PR Newswire, October 20, 2021. https://mediablog.prnewswire.com/2021/10/20/ai-in-the-newsroom-these-outlets-arent-spooked.

6. Parker.

7. Julian Dosset. "Where AI may take journalism in 2019." PR Newswire, updated September 23, 2021. https://mediablog.prnewswire.com/2018/11/20/where-artificial-intelligence-may-take-journalism-in-2019/.

8. Carrie Teegardin and Danny Robbins. "Still Forgiven." *Atlanta Journal-Constitution*, n.d. https://doctors.ajc.com.

9. Nicholas Diakopoulos. "AI in the Newsroom." Podcast. This is one of many findings cited in this chapter, originating from sources retrieved from https://datajournalism.com/read/newsletters/ai-in-the-newsroom.

10. CNBC Television channel. "World's first AI news anchor debuts in China." YouTube video, posted November 9, 2018. https://www.youtube.com/watch?v=MHPI1uH9llU.

11. Dosset.

12. "A robot wrote this entire article. Are you scared yet, human?" *The Guardian*, September 8, 2020. All citations related to the *Guardian*'s AI-written editorial were retrieved from https://www.theguardian.com/commentisfree/2020/sep/08/robot-wrote-this-article-gpt-3.

Chapter 4

1. Tiffany Hsu and Yiwen Lu. "A Blessing and a Boogeyman: Advertisers warily embrace AI." *New York Times*, July 18, 2023. https://www.nytimes.com/2023/07/18/business/media/ai-advertising.html.

2. Elliot Wiser. "Shifting Newsroom Economics." In *Journalism and the Pandemic: Essays on Innovation and Adaptation*, Tony Silvia, ed. (McFarland, 2022), 137–147.

3. Megan Graham. "How a stay at home year accelerated three trends in the advertising industry." CNBC, March 13, 2021. https://www.cnbc.com/2021/03/13/how-covid-19-changed-the-advertising-industry-.html.

4. Graham.

5. Eddie Kim. "AI's disruption in newsrooms." Memo, April 25, 2023. https://memo.co/blog/ais-disruption-in-newsrooms.

6. Arthur Sants. "How media companies can react to the AI boom." Investors' Chronicle, July 26, 2023. https://www.investorschronicle.co.uk/news/2023/07/26/how-media-companies-can-react-to-the-ai-boom/.

7. Richard Tofel. "It's the First Budget Season of the AI Revolution." Second Rough Draft, July 13, 2023. https://dicktofel.substack.com/p/its-the-first-budget-season-of-the.

8. Simplilearn. "How Netflix uses AI, Data, Science, and ML." Simplilearn, November 7, 2023. https://www.simplilearn.com/how-netflix-uses-ai-data-science-and-ml-article.

9. "Machine Learning: Learning how to entertain the world." Netflix, accessed November 2023. https://research.netflix.com/research-area/machine-learning.

10. https://www.digitalfirst.ai/blog/use-cases-and-examples-of-ai-digital-marketing.

11. Hsu and Lu.

12. Isabelle Vanderheiden. "Humboldt supervisors to consider revocation." Lost Coast Outpost, September 25, 2023. https://lostcoastoutpost.com/agendizer/humboldt-county-supes/224.

13. Sophie Culpepper. "Can AI help local newsrooms streamline their newsletters? ARLnow tests the waters." NiemanLab, May 8, 2023. https://www.niemanlab.org/2023/05/can-ai-help-local-newsrooms-streamline-their-newsletters-arlnow-tests-the-waters/.

14. John Zhang. "Why are AI models getting cheaper as they improve?" Technode, March 27, 2023. https://technode.com/2023/03/27/why-are-ai-models-getting-cheaper-as-they-improve/.

15. "Journalism AI." London School of Economics. https://www.lse.ac.uk/media-and-communications/polis/JournalismAI, accessed April 2024.

16. Abdel El Ouazzani. "5 ways AI personalization can increase revenues." Kameleoon, September 26, 2019. https://www.kameleoon.com/en/blog/5-ways-ai-personalization-can-increase-media-revenues. All previous and subsequent references to this study are from this source.

17. Ouazzani.

18. Chinmayi Bettadapur. "3 ways media companies can use AI to find a new revenue." The 360 Blog, Salesforce, July 27, 2023. https://www.salesforce.com/blog/media-revenue-ai/. All references to the Salesforce strategy regarding

AI, previous and subsequent, are taken from this source.

Chapter 5

1. Averi Harper, et al. "Political campaigns raising red flags into 2024 election." ABC News, November 8, 2023. https://abcnews.go.com/Politics/ai-political-campaigns-raising-red-flags-2024-election/story?id=102480464. All references to the ABC news stories on this topic are from this source.
2. Claire Duffy. "Google to require disclosures of AI content in political ads." CNN Business, September 8, 2023. https://www.cnn.com/2023/09/08/tech/google-political-ad-policy-ai-content/index.html.
3. David Klepper. "To help 2024 voters, Meta says it will begin labeling political ads that use AI-generated imagery." Associated Press, November 8, 2023. https://apnews.com/article/meta-facebook-instagram-political-ads-deepfakes-2024-c4aec653d5043a09b1c78b4fb5dcd79b.
4. Catherine Powell and Alexandra Dent. "Artificial Intelligence Enters the Political Arena." Council on Foreign Relations, May 24, 2023. https://www.cfr.org/blog/artificial-intelligence-enters-political-arena.
5. Robert Chesney and Danielle Citron. "Deepfakes and the New Information War." *Foreign Affairs*, December 11, 2018. https://www.foreignaffairs.com/articles/world/2018-12-11/deepfakes-and-new-disinformation-war. See also Josh Goldstein and Girish Sastry, "The Coming Age of AI-Powered Propaganda," for additional perspective. *Foreign Affairs*, April 7, 2023. https://www.foreignaffairs.com/united-states/coming-age-ai-powered-propaganda.
6. Huo Jingnan. "AI-generated text is hard to spot. It could play a big role in the 2024 campaign." NPR, June 29, 2023. https://www.npr.org/2023/06/29/1183684732/ai-generated-text-is-hard-to-spot-it-could-play-a-big-role-in-the-2024-campaign.
7. Darrell West. "How to combat fake news and disinformation." Brookings, December 18, 2017. https://www.brookings.edu/articles/how-to-combat-fake-news-and-disinformation/.
8. Sabrina Siddiqui and Ryan Tracy. "AI's Rapid Growth Threatens to Flood 2024 Campaigns with Fake Videos." *Wall Street Journal*, June 5, 2023. https://www.wsj.com/articles/ais-rapid-growth-threatens-to-flood-2024-campaigns-with-fake-videos-dbd8144f.
9. Clay Calvert. "AI gets political: how do we keep fake news out of campaign ads?" The Hill, June 13, 2023. https://thehill.com/opinion/technology/4046406-ai-gets-political-how-do-we-keep-fake-news-out-of-campaign-ads.
10. Patrick Howe, et al. "Exploring Reporter-Desired Features for an AI-Generated Legislative News Tip Sheet." *International Society of Journalists Journal* 12(1) (2022): 17–44. https://isoj.org/research/exploring-reporter-desired-features-for-an-ai-generated-legislative-news-tip-sheet/. Subsequent quotations regarding this topic are from this source.

Chapter 6

1. Marina Fridman, Roy Krøvel, and Fabrizio Palumbo. "How (Not to) Run an AI Project in Investigative Journalism." *Journalism Practice*, September 2023, 1–18. doi:10.1080/17512786.2023.2253797.
2. Monika Sengul-Jones. "How machine learning can analyze massive data sets to unearth untold stories." DataJournalism, December 1, 2021. https://datajournalism.com/read/longreads/machine-learning-investigative-journalism.
3. Fridman, Krøvel, and Palumbo.
4. International Consortium of Investigative Journalists. "Giant Leak of Offshore Financial Records Exposes Global Array of Crime and Corruption." ICIJ, April 3, 2016. https://www.icij.org/investigations/panama-papers/20160403-panama-papers-global-overview/.
5. Charlie Beckett. "The Impact of

AI and Collaboration on Investigative Journalism." London School of Economics, April 8, 2020. https://blogs.lse.ac.uk/polis/2020/04/08/the-impact-of-ai-and-collaboration-on-investigative-journalism/

6. Beckett.

7. Simon Bowers. "Leaked Documents Expose Secret Tale of Apple's Offshore Island Hop." ICIJ, November 8, 2017. https://www.icij.org/investigations/paradise-papers/apples-secret-offshore-island-hop-revealed-by-paradise-papers-leak-icij/.

8. Bowers.

9. Fabiola Torres Lopez. "How They Did It: Methods and Tools Used to Investigate the Paradise Papers." Global Investigative Journalism Network, December 4, 2017. https://gijn.org/stories/paradise-papers/.

10. Beckett.

11. Beckett.

12. Danny Robbins et al. "How the Doctors & Sex Abuse project came about." *Atlanta Journal-Constitution.* https://doctors.ajc.com/about_this_investigation, accessed November 2023.

13. Peter Aldhous. "We Trained a Computer to Search for Hidden Spy Planes. This Is What It Found." Buzz-Feed News, August 7, 2017. https://www.buzzfeednews.com/article/peteraldhous/hidden-spy-planes.

14. Robin Guess. "How AI Could Act as Boost for Investigative Journalism." VOA News, January 10, 2024. https://www.voanews.com/a/how-ai-could-act-as-boost-for-investigative-journalism/7434364.html.

15. Laura Oliver. "AI Journalism Lessons from a 150-Year-Old Argentinian Newspaper." Global Investigative Journalism Network, February 22, 2022. https://gijn.org/resource/ai-journalism-lessons-from-a-150-year-old-argentinian-newspaper/. All references in this part of the discussion are from this source.

Chapter 7

1. The Associated Press regularly revisits and updates its guidelines on the use of social media. The latest version of its policy: https://www.ap.org/assets/documents/social-media-guidelines_tcm28-9832.pdf.

2. Jeffrey Gottfried, et al. "Many journalists say social media helps at work, but most decry its impact on journalism." Pew Research Center, June 14, 2022. https://www.pewresearch.org/journalism/2022/06/14/many-journalists-say-social-media-helps-at-work-but-most-decry-its-impact-on-journalism/.

3. https://www.ap.org/assets/documents/social-media-guidelines_tcm28-9832.pdf.

4. AIContentfy Team. "The rise of AI-generated social media posts." AIContentfy, June 27, 2024. https://aicontentfy.com/en/blog/rise-of-ai-generated-social-media-posts.

5. Emma Colton. "AI appears more human on social media than actual humans: study." Fox News, July 25, 2023. https://www.foxnews.com/tech/ai-appears-more-human-social-media-than-actual-humans-study.

6. Caitlin Chin-Rothmann. "Navigating the Risks of Artificial Intelligence on the Digital News Landscape." Center for Strategic and International Studies, August 31, 2023. https://www.csis.org/analysis/navigating-risks-artificial-intelligence-digital-news-landscape. All subsequent references to this study are from this source.

7. The results of this second study are summarized throughout this section from the aforementioned article cited from https://aicontentfy.com/en/blog/rise-of-ai-generated-social-media-posts.

Chapter 8

1. Euronews. "News organisations are using AI, but many are concerned about its ethical implacations, survey shows." Euronews, September 20, 2023. https://www.euronews.com/next/2023/09/20/news-organisations-are-using-ai-but-many-are-concerned-about-its-ethical-implications-surv.

2. Bernat Ivancsics and Mark Hansen.

Chapter Notes

"Actually, it's about Ethics, AI, and Journalism: Reporting on and with Computation and Data." *Columbia Journalism Review*, Tow Report, November 21, 2019. https://www.cjr.org/tow_center_reports/ai-ethics-journalism-and-computation-ibm-new-york-times.php. All references to the Tow report and its conclusions are derived from this source.

3. Charlotte Tobbit. "The ethics of using generative AI to create journalism: What we know so far." PressGazette, April 18, 2023. https://pressgazette.co.uk/publishers/digital-journalism/ai-news-journalism-ethics/.

4. Society of Professional Journalists (SPJ) Code of Ethics, revised September 6, 2014. https://www.spj.org/ethicscode.asp.

5. The Thomson Foundation. "Paris Charter on AI and Journalism unveiled." Thomson Foundation. https://www.thomsonfoundation.org/latest/paris-charter-on-ai-and-journalism-unveiled, accessed February 4, 2024. All previous, present, and subsequent citations to this report derive from this source.

6. Vincent Peyrègne. "Global Principles for Artificial Intelligence." World Association of News Publishers, September 6, 2023. https://wan-ifra.org/insight/global-principles-for-artificial-intelligence/.

7. WAN-IFRA Staff. "Charter for AI and Journalism: tech standards must be the responsibility of publishers." World Association of News Publishers, November 19, 2023. https://wan-ifra.org/2023/11/wan-ifra-steps-back-from-endorsing-new-charter-for-ai-and-journalism/.

8. "Journalism, AI, and ethics." *Cedar Valley Sentinel*. https://cedarvalleysentinel.com/journalism-ai-and-ethics, accessed February 20, 2024. All previous and subsequent references to the publication's AI policies are derived from this source.

9. Editors, *Wired*. "How WIRED will use AI tools." *Wired*. https://www.wired.com/about/generative-ai-policy, accessed February 28, 2024. All previous and subsequent references to the publication's AI policies are derived from this source.

10. RTNDA. "Use of Artificial Intelligence (AI) in Journalism." Radio Television Digital News Association. https://www.rtdna.org/use-of-ai-in-journalism, accessed March 2, 2024.

11. Adriana Lacy. "Ethical considerations in AI journalism." Adriana Lacy Consulting, January 3, 2024. https://blog.adrianalacyconsulting.com/ethical-considerations-ai-journalism/.

12. Sara Fischer. "OpenAI funds new journalism ethics initiative." Axios, August 8, 2023. https://www.axios.com/2023/08/08/openai-journalism-ethics-nyu.

13. Charlotte Tobitt. "The ethics of using generative AI to create journalism: What we know so far." PressGazette, April 17, 2023. https://pressgazette.co.uk/publishers/digital-journalism/ai-news-journalism-ethics.

14. Tobitt.

15. Quoted in Tobitt.

16. Shannon Bond. "AI-generated deepfakes are moving fast, policy makers can't keep up." NPR, April 27, 2023. https://www.npr.org/2023/04/27/1172387911/how-can-people-spot-fake-images-created-by-artificial-intelligence.

17. Philip Marcelo. "Fake image of Pentagon explosion briefly sends jitters through stock market." Associated Press, May 23, 2023. https://apnews.com/article/pentagon-explosion-misinformation-stock-market-ai-96f534c790872fde67012ee81b5ed6a4.

18. Bond.

19. Deanna Ritchie. "Deepfakes: AI-generated images that went viral in 2023." Readwrite, December 24, 2023. https://readwrite.com/deepfake-ai-generated-images-that-went-viral-in-2023.

20. Quoted in Bond.

21. ChatGPT, an experiment conducted by the author on January 16, 2024.

22. While the outcome is fictional, this is an actual book that I wrote: *Journalism and the Pandemic: Essays on Adaptation and Innovation* (McFarland, 2022).

Chapter 9

1. National Inventors Hall of Fame. "Guglielmo Marconi." Marconi was

inducted in 1975. https://www.invent.
org/inductees/guglielmo-marconi.

2. TCL Guides. "Who Invented Television: History of TV." *TCL Guides*,
June 28, 2023. Its inventor is generally
accepted to have been Philo T. Farn-
sworth. https://www.tcl.com/global/en/
blog/playbooks/history-of-tv.

3. Online Library Learning Center.
"A Brief History of the Internet." University System of Georgia. https://www.usg.
edu/galileo/skills/unit07/internet07_02.
phtml.

4. Tanya Roy. "The History and Evolution of Artificial Intelligence, AI's
Present and Future."*AllTech Magazine*,
July 19, 2023. https://alltechmagazine.
com/the-evolution-of-ai.

5. Steve Henn. "Remembering When
Driverless Elevators Drew Skepticism."
NPR, July 31, 2015. https://www.npr.org/
2015/07/31/427990392/remembering-wh
en-driverless-elevators-drew-skepticism.

6. Sarah Kessler. "Automation anxiety dates back to the late 16 century." Quartz, August 12, 2019. https://
qz.com/1681832/the-history-of-the-
future-of-work.

7. His extended biography can be
found at https://jacobward.com/about-
me/.

8. Zoom interview conducted by the
author in February, 2024. All quotations
are from that interview.

9. His extended biography can be
found at https://davidpogue.com/about/.

10. Zoom interview conducted by the
author in February, 2024. All quotations
are from that interview.

11. Pogue also extends his assertion
about deep fakes to the political arena
here: https://www.instagram.com/reel/
C7W27ipB5eJ/.

12. For more on his background,
see https://www.usf.edu/arts-sciences/
departments/journalism/people/faculty-
and-staff/stephen-song.aspx.

13. Zoom interview conducted by the
author in March 2024. All quotations are
from that interview.

14. For his extended biography, see
https://www.poynter.org/author/tony-
elkins/.

15. Zoom interview conducted by the
author in March 2024. All quotations are
from that interview.

16. This quotation arose from conversation during a podcast conducted by the
author in June 2023. Bill Whitaker con-
tributed the foreword to *Journalism and
the Pandemic: Essays on Adaptation and
Innovation* (McFarland, 2022).

17. The section that follows tracks
the questions and responses from the
author's prompts to ChatGPT in February 2024.

Suggestions for
Further Reading

The following is a select list of publications related to the topic of artificial intelligence in journalism and media in general.

Books

Biswal, Sandmarsh, and Arand Kalkarni. *Exploring the Intersection of Artificial Intelligence and Journalism*. Routledge, 2024.

Giansiracusa, Noah. *How Algorithms Create and Prevent Fake News: Exploring the Impacts of Social Media, Deepfakes, GPT-3, and More*. Apress, 2021.

Latar, Noam. *Robot Journalism: Can Human Journalism Survive*. World Scientific, 2018.

Marconi, Francesco. *Artificial Intelligence and the Future of Journalism*. Columbia University Press, 2020.

Min, Seong Jae. *Rethinking the New Technology of Journalism: How Slowing Down Will Save the News*. Penn State University Press, 2022.

Natale, Simone. *Deceitful Media: Artificial Intelligence and Social Life After the Turing Test*. Oxford University Press, 2021.

Pihlajarinne, Taina, and Anette Alen-Savikko, eds. *Artificial Intelligence and the Media: Reconsidering Rights and Responsibilities*. Elgar Publishing, 2022

Sterling, Maxwell. *Artificial Intelligence: Navigating the AI Revolution: A Beginner's Guide to Understanding AI*. Independently published, 2024.

Ward, Jacob. *The Loop: How Technology is Creating a World Without Choices and How to Fight Back*. Hachette, 2022.

Wishart, Eric. *Journalism Ethics:21 Essentials from Wars to Artificial Intelligence*. Hong Kong University Press, 2024.

Whitaker, Jason Paul. *Tech Giants, Artificial Intelligence, and the Future of Journalism*. Routledge, 2019.

Articles

Annor, Ignatius. "Is artificial intelligence a threat to journalism?" Voice of America, May 2, 2023. https://www.voaafrica.com/a/is-artificial-intelligence-a-threat-to-journalism-/7070199.html.

Bhaimiya, Sawdah. "If you fell for the AI generated image of Pope Francis, here are the tell-tale signs." *Business Insider*, March 27, 2023. https://www.businessinsider.com/viral-image-pope-francis-generated-by-ai-fooled-social-media-2023-3.

Brown, Craig. "Can robots learn to do journalism?" *The Columbian*, March 11, 2023. https://www.columbian.com/news/2023/mar/11/from-the-newsroom-can-robots-learn-to-do-journalism.

Suggestions for Further Reading

Conley, Julia. "Fake content industry, AI pose threat to fact-based journalism worldwide." Common Dreams, May 3, 2023. https://www.commondreams.org/news/fake-content-ai-threat-journalism.

Darrach, Amanda. "The threat to photojournalism no one is talking about." *Columbia Journalism Review*, March 1, 2023. https://www.cjr.org/the_media_today/fred_ritchin_ai_photojournalism.php.

Duffy, Claire. "Fake AI news images are fooling social media users." CNN, April 3, 2023. https://www.cnn.com/2023/04/02/tech/ai-generated-images-social-media/index.html.

Dupré, Maggie Harrison. "Guy launches news site that's completely generated by AI." Futurism, May 3, 2023. https://futurism.com/news-site-completely-generated-ai.

Elliott, Victoria, and Makena Kelly. "The Biden deepfake robocall is only the beginning" *Wired*, January 23, 2024. https://www.wired.com/story/biden-robocall-deepfake-danger/.

Fahri, Paul. "A news site used AI to write news articles. It was a journalistic disaster." *Washington Post*, January 17, 2023. https://www.washingtonpost.com/media/2023/01/17/cnet-ai-articles-journalism-corrections/.

From Above Team. "Journalists' guide to using AI and satellite Imagery for Storytelling." Global Investigative Journalists Network, February 16, 2022. https://gijn.org/2022/02/16/journalists-guide-to-using-ai-and-satellite-imagery-for-storytelling/.

Hermida, Alfred. "Artificial Intelligence and journalism." *Policy Options*, February 1, 2018. https://policyoptions.irpp.org/magazines/february-2018/artificial-intelligence-and-journalism/.

Hsu, Tiffany. "Can we no longer believe anything we see?" *New York Times*, April 8, 2023. https://www.nytimes.com/2023/04/08/business/media/ai-generated-images.html.

Kahn, Gretel. "Will AI generated images create a new crisis for fact checkers?" Reuters Institute, April 11, 2023. https://reutersinstitute.politics.ox.ac.uk/news/will-ai-generated-images-create-new-crisis-fact-checkers-are-not-so-sure.

Keefe, John, Youyou Zhou, and Jeremy B. Merrill. "The present and potential of AI in journalism." Knight Foundation, May 12, 2021. https://knightfoundation.org/articles/the-present-and-potential-of-ai-in-journalism/.

Lacy, Adriana. "AI newsroom revolution: ethical considerations in AI journalism." Adriana Lacy Consulting, January 3, 2024. https://blog.adrianalacyconsulting.com/ethical-considerations-ai-journalism/.

Landymore, Frank. "CNET is quietly publishing entire articles generated by AI." Futurism, January 15, 2023. https://futurism.com/the-byte/cnet-publishing-articles-by-ai.

Le Grand, Heloise. "How to use artificial intelligence without losing audience trust." International Center for Journalists, June 14, 2023. https://www.icfj.org/news/how-use-artificial-intelligence-journalism-without-losing-audience-trust.

Lippolis, Anna Sophia, and Jakob Parusinski. "What AI image generators can do for newsrooms." The Fix, October 20, 2022. https://thefix.media/2022/10/20/what-ai-image-generators-can-do-for-newsrooms.

McBride, Kelly. "Your newsroom needs an AI ethics policy. Start here." Poynter Institute, March 25, 2024. https://www.poynter.org/ethics-trust/2024/how-to-create-newsroom-artificial-intelligence-ethics-policy/.

McKendrick, Joe. "As AI Rapidly Becomes a Commodity, Time to Consider the Next Step." *Forbes*, February 7, 2024. https://www.forbes.com/sites/joemckendrick/2024/02/07/as-ai-rapidly-becomes-a-commodity-time-to-consider-the-next-step/.

Merrefield, Clark. "Researchers compare AI policies at 52 news organizations around the world." Journalist's Resource, December 12, 2023. https://journalistsresource.org/home/generative-ai-policies-newsrooms/.

Roy, Ishita. "Will artificial intelligence make journalists obsolete?" *India Times*, March

9, 2023. https://www.indiatimes.com/explainers/news/will-artificial-intelligence-make-journalists-obsolete-595026.html.

Scanlan, Chip, and Casey Frechette. "Two journalists talk to the bots, who talk back, about the pros and pitfalls of AI." *Nieman Storyboard*, February 16, 2024. https://niemanstoryboard.org/stories/journalism-ethics-artificial-intelligence-sources-fact-checking/.

Shafer, Jack. "How AI is already transforming the news business." *Politico*, February 27, 2024. https://www.politico.com/news/magazine/2024/02/27/artificial-intelligence-media-00143508.

Sher, Gai, and Ariela Benchlouch. "The privacy paradox with AI." Reuters, October 31, 2023. https://www.reuters.com/legal/legalindustry/privacy-paradox-with-ai-2023-10-31/.

Society of Professional Journalists. "AI tools for journalists." Journalist's Toolbox, May 25, 2023. https://www.journaliststoolbox.org/2023/05/08/ai-tools-for-journalists/.

Villa, Santiago. "Investigating—and embracing—the AI revolution." Global Investigative Journalism Network, September 20, 2023. https://gijn.org/stories/ai-and-investigative-journalism-gijc23/.

INDEX

Index